Trees of Life

Trees of Life

THE PRAYER OF INTERCESSION
AND ITS COST

Una Kroll

DRAWINGS BY REBECCA ABREY

MOWBRAY

Mowbray
A Cassell imprint
Wellington House, 125 Strand, London WC2R 0BB
PO Box 605, Herndon, VA 20172

First published 1997

Unless otherwise stated, scriptural quotations are from the New Revised Standard Version, ©
1989, 1995 Division of Christian Education of the National Council of the Churches of Christ
in the United States of America.

British Library Cataloguing-in-Publication Data
A catalogue record for this book is available from the British Library.

ISBN 0-264-67452-9

Typeset by BookEns Ltd, Royston, Herts.
Printed and bound in Great Britain by
Biddles Ltd, Guildford and King's Lynn

For The Companions
of
Jesus Crucified

Contents

Part Three   The fruits of intercession

Acknowledgements

In preparing this book I am grateful to all the people who have accompanied me on the journey of prayer, especially to my husband Leo, my spiritual director, Fr Donald Allchin, my friends, Sr Marie Greene RSHM, Srs Joan Scott and Maraid Quigley RSCJ, and Donald Nicholl.

I am again grateful to the Revd James Coutts, my vicar, for his 'one-minute' theological reflections which so many of us find challenging and life-giving.

Acknowledgements are due to the following for permission to quote copyright material: A. & C. Black Ltd (Iulia de Beausobre, *Creative Suffering*); Burns & Oates (Ida Görres, *The Hidden Face*); Carcanet (Elizabeth Jennings, *Times and Seasons*); Church Mission Society (prayer from *Morning Noon and Night*, ed. John Carden); Constable (Iulia de Beausobre, *Flame in the Snow*); Darton, Longman and Todd (Julian Shrine, *Enfolded in Love* and Kathryn Spink, *The Call of the Desert*); Hawthorne Books (Alf McCreary, *Corrymeela: Hill of Harmony*); Hodder & Stoughton (Mary Craig, *Candles in the Dark* and Elizabeth Hamilton, *The Desert My Dwelling Place*); Gerald Hudson ('Gethsemene'); Ignatius Press (Adrienne von Speyr, *Confession*); *David Jones, Drawings and Paintings*; Le Livre Ouvert (Little Sister Magdeleine of Jesus, *Jesus Is the Master of the Impossible*); Marshall Pickering (Joni Eareckson Tada, *Start of a Journey*); New City (Olivier Clément, *The Roots of Christian Mysticism*); Penguin Books (Michael Alexander, *Earliest English Poems*); *The Tablet* (Michael Alexander, *Ancient Witness to the Crucifixion* and Monks of St Bernard, *Statement of Murdered Trappist Abbot*); Veritas Publications (Maria Tarnawska, *Blessed Sister Faustina*).

Every effort has been made to trace copyright holders; if any holder has been overlooked, the publishers would be glad to hear, so that acknowledgement may be made in any future editions of this book.

Alpha

The seed is carried
on the wings of
the dove of peace,
then dropped
in the place
designed.

The hard husk
yields
to its purpose:
guards
the living
germ within
until the time
decreed by God.

Then,
only then,
the husk
breaks open,
and dies.
The roots
break forth
reaching deep
into God's soil.

And grow.

We cannot see
what will be;
only what is.
Pray to God
that the seed
falls upon
good ground
and yields
a hundred-fold.

Pray.

Quercus robur. A sturdy hardwood tree that lives to a great age.

The boundary oak

In an East Sussex garden there is an old oak tree that marks the boundary between two properties.

I was six years old when I first came to see my uncle's new property, but I did not immediately notice the oak. My older cousin and I were intent on searching for a stream that lay at the very bottom of a tangled copse of small beech and hazel trees that led steeply down towards the sound of running water.

We soon found what we were looking for. We would spend many happy hours by that running water in the future, but on this, the first day in our new holiday home, we did not linger. Turning, we made our way up through the thicket again. As we came out into the clear rough-grassed field, I saw the oak far over on the right side of the slope. It stood alone by a dividing wire fence. It must have stood there for hundreds of years, judging by its size, but I did not then know anything about the growth of trees. All I knew was that the oak tree felt like a friend. I ran towards it as fast as my small legs would allow me to move.

'It's very old', my cousin said.

'It isn't; it's my friend, and you can't have friends who are grown up.'

'You are so silly; you can't make friends with a tree.' My cousin stalked off to find her parents.

'I can', I said to myself, putting my hand on the bark of the tree, 'and I'll come here and tell you all my secrets', I added, as I leant against its solid and comforting trunk.

At the end of our summer holidays we returned to our homes in the city of London, but, wherever I went between visits, I always thought of that place as my home, and the tree as my friend. The next time I came there I went straight to it. It was still there, presiding watchfully over changes that had overtaken the whole area since my first visit. Now there was a wooden bungalow on the property. In front of it there was the beginning of a lawn with three rose beds in it. The oak tree had been shut off from the garden by a holly hedge on one side and sloe trees and a cypress hedge on the other side. I went through a gap between the hedges to reach it. My uncle was there.

'It's my chopping and burning place now', he said as I reached the tree.

Looking round I saw that the dark stamped-down ground in front of the tree had become a bonfire site. Small branches and grass cuttings were piled up in the clearing ready to be set alight on the next dry and windless day. An axe lay against the tree trunk. A great pile of leaves had been put against its far side.

'That's my compost heap', my uncle said. 'It's damp here and those leaves will make a good mulch for the garden next year.'

I stood still and silent. My tree, my friend, was now next to an enclosed and rather dark space for burning garden refuse, a space that would echo to the sound of living branches being chopped into logs. It would become a place where compost was produced out of dank leaves and smelly kitchen refuse.

'I'll still love you', I whispered. 'I'll still come here and talk to you whenever I can.'

And I did: all the way through adolescence and into early adult life. When I became a grown woman, a mother and a grandmother, the oak tree took on new significance in my life. I rejoiced when my children used my beloved tree, and many others too, as climbing frames, sources of food, exciting places under which to find small insects, mushrooms, wood anemones and wild cyclamen. I mourned when rain forests were felled, when elm trees died of disease, when terrible gales swept through my country and toppled tall firs and cypresses, when a garden tree had to be chopped down because its old age had rendered it unsafe. I retained my love of my own special oak tree and extended it to many species, indeed to all God's creation.

My life kept me away for long periods of time, but over the years I was able to return at intervals to my childhood home, and to the oak tree. Eventually the land was sold. I will never see the oak tree again and yet it has remained alive in my memory as a place of safety, stability and secrecy.

For many years now I have been reflecting on the significance of trees in relation to the Christian life. They are rooted in God's earth from which they draw the water that sustains their life. Trees give delight through their variety. They grow at different rates and in a myriad of ways. They bear distinctive leaves, flowers and fruit. Each has a specific purpose in God's creation. Trees grow towards the sky; they stretch high to find the sunlight and air they need to live and do their work of glorifying God. I find in them attributes that echo within my own life and those of other people as they become rooted in Christ, grow through grace and reach towards heaven to find their glory.

In the Judaeo-Christian Scriptures trees are sometimes used as symbols and metaphors. So, for instance, there are references to the tree of life, the tree of the knowledge of good and evil, the life-giving tree of the cross and the tree that spans the river of the water of life. The tree in the garden of a child's memory has some of its roots in the real trees of the Bible, the oaks of Mamre, the tree whose forked branch held Absalom tight in its grip until he was slain, and the olive trees of the garden of Gethsemene. The solid stability of a tree's presence in the heart of a small child has its counterpart in the garden of Eden and on the rood where the new Adam died to bring us life, that same living tree whose leaves are for the healing of the nations.

Thoughts about trees, both those that are real and those that are symbols, have woven themselves into my life. This book is the outcome of reflection on the Scriptures as they resonate with a lifetime's experience of prayer. It is about one kind of prayer — intercession, or petitionary prayer. It is about people who come to Christ with concerns that they ask him to lay before his Creator and theirs. Intercession takes the Christian disciple to the heart of Christ's cosmic work on the cross and unites his suffering to ours, and ours to his, his victory to ours, and ours to his. Any author must approach such a subject with awe and trembling, yet also try to incarnate the mystery in words that give meaning to experience.

Each of the first three chapters begins with a personal true story about a tree that illustrates some qualities that Christians need to develop if they are to pray to their heavenly Father from within the mind of Christ. In these chapters some of the problems that intercessors often encounter are discussed.

The next three chapters also begin with a real-life story about a tree. They portray the way in which human beings are sometimes called by God to be involved in specific kinds of petitionary prayer. These chapters focus in turn on healing prayer that is linked to Christ's wounds, reconciling prayer that has its roots in Christ's atoning work on the cross, and prayer for unity between all people that is faithful to Christ's high priestly prayer, 'that they may be one, as we are one' (John 17.21 and 23).

The last two chapters and their tree stories are about the fruits of intercession and the victory that Christ has already won for us by his passion, death, resurrection and ascension.

The same method is used in each chapter. Each story is followed by thoughts that relate experience to the word of God in the Bible and in the teachings of the Christian Church. These reflections are followed by some practical suggestions that might be of help not only to intercessors but to those who accompany them on their journey as 'soul friends', spiritual directors and companions.

Part One

The call to intercession

Aesculus hippocastanum. The horse chestnut.

A beautiful deciduous soft wood
tree bearing shiny brown
nuts encased in
prickly green shells.

1

The willow tree and the chestnut tree

ROOTING PRAYER IN CHRIST

Then God said, 'Let the earth put forth vegetation: plants yielding seed, and fruit trees of every kind on earth that bear fruit with the seed in it.' And it was so. (Genesis 1.11)

> Blessed are those who trust in the Lord,
>   whose trust is the Lord.
> They shall be like a tree planted by water,
>   sending out its roots by the stream.
> It shall not fear when heat comes,
>   and its leaves shall stay green;
> in the year of drought it is not anxious,
>   and it does not cease to bear fruit. (Jeremiah 17.7–8)

When I was an undergraduate medical student, I loved to lie under the shade of the willow trees by the banks of the river in Cambridge. I would lie there for hours with a textbook at hand: I would read a page or two before allowing my eyes to dwell on the river bank where the surface roots seemed to thrust themselves into the water. The passing punts made the river water slap against the roots; sometimes the drooping branches would shiver in the breeze created by the wind or by the motion of the boats and their student cargo.

I had recently become a Christian. The rich poetry of the Bible was enjoyable; moreover, it was easy to make connections between the Cambridge willow trees and the trees by the riverside in the prophecies of Jeremiah, together with its parallel passage in the first psalm. It was sometimes possible to think of others, though not, at that point, of myself, as like trees thrusting their roots down into the water of life, Christ himself.

One day, however, I was confronted with a very different image. I was invited into a garden where many years ago someone had fastened a metal figure of Christ to the trunk of a young chestnut tree. The tree had continued to grow. In time its bark and phloem had grown around the figure; by now it had become embedded in the soft wood and could not have been removed without inflicting damage.

When I first saw it there, I felt affronted for the tree. It had been wounded by a human being for the sake of making a point — that Christ died on a tree — 'a point', I thought, 'that everyone knows'. When my immediate anger died down, and I could think more rationally, I began to look more closely at the relationship between the figure of Jesus and the living tree. I translated the metal figure into the living figure of Christ. I began to see the tree as a metaphor for a living person. Once I had done that, I saw another 'point' I had not previously seen. It did not come to me immediately: I had to work it out.

As a youngster I had found out that a child can easily talk to a tree as a friend. He or she can also talk to Jesus in quite intimate ways. Jesus has a human face; he can be seen in pictures, statues and stained-glass windows in churches. To a small boy or girl it becomes quite natural to think of mummy and daddy, Jesus and Father God, in the same breath. Talking to him is much like talking to a parent. This is how many children in Christian families learn to pray.

One of the first things they are taught is to speak to God in their own words: 'Thank you, God, for my mummy and daddy; please take care of them.' 'Please look after my granny who is ill.' Later, they add contrition to these prayers of thanksgiving and supplication: 'Dear God, I'm sorry that I was rude to my teacher.' Adoration of God usually comes later when the awareness of beauty moves an older child or adolescent to prayer. Often it is the beauty of nature that stirs a lively heart to praise God. Sometimes it is sheer wonder, the kind of wonder that can happen when boy or girl sees a newborn younger brother or sister for the first time.

Young children in Christian families are often taught to say the Lord's prayer, 'Abba, Father' (Matthew 6.9–13) by heart without understanding what they are saying. This prayer is, of course, central to all Christian life and worship. It is the pattern for all intercessory prayer, as will be seen later in this chapter.

Many adult Christians continue to pray as they did when they were small children. They pray with simplicity and confidence. They use familiar words; they find a pattern of adoration, contrition, thanksgiving and supplication, and they stay with it. Some people, however, find that as they mature they find that when they read Scripture they adopt its metaphors almost unconsciously. They may also develop an ability to identify with images; these become symbols of reality for them.

When, as a nineteen-year-old medical student, I saw that the willow trees by the bank of the river Cam were related to the person whom Jeremiah described as being 'like a tree planted by water, sending out its roots by the stream' (Jeremiah 17.8), I could make the connection between trees and human beings. It was the first move towards an ability to identify myself with the living chestnut tree that enclosed a metal figure that I suddenly saw to be the living person of Christ dwelling in me and in other people.

In the years that have followed, this understanding has been expanded by reading the Scriptures and seeing in them theological truth that adds objectivity to experience. Anyone who reads the books of the Bible can find an obvious theological connection between the tree of life, the tree of the knowledge of good and evil, the tree of the cross and the salvation of humankind. These trees are used as metaphors that help to explain the mystery of our salvation. Their role in intercessory prayer will be discussed in later chapters.

In this chapter, however, it is the ordinary trees that crowd the pages of the Bible that help me to explore the relationship between trees and human beings, people and their Creator, Christians and Christ.

By the time the earliest books of the Old Testament were composed, trees had already existed for millions of years. It was in the Devonian age, 165 million years ago, that God created a tree, a ginkgo tree,[1] and saw that it was good. Many more millions of years were to pass before human beings were created. By then the earth was clad with rich vegetation and many species of trees, deciduous and coniferous.

The commonplace trees of the Bible appear in a profuse variety of species, habitat and use. Their primary purpose in God's creation is that of producing shelter, nesting places, leaves whose respiration helps to maintain the oxygen content of the air, flowers and fruit that can be used for food and medicines. Trees are also seen as places of encounter with God (Genesis 18.1), of shelter and rest during the hottest part of the day (Genesis 18.4) and of hospitality (Genesis 18.8). They were also used as places of execution (Genesis 40.19). Nevertheless, the predominant note throughout the Old Testament is that trees exist to glorify God. Many writers use them in positive and lyrical ways. So, for instance, the psalmist sings in praise of creation:

> The trees of the Lord are watered abundantly,
>   the cedars of Lebanon that he planted.
> In them the birds build their nests,
>   the stork has its home in the fir trees. (Psalm 104.16–17)

The writer of the Song of Songs uses the image of a forest in springtime to speak of the climate in which love flourishes:

> The flowers appear on the earth.
>   The time of singing has come,
> and the voice of the turtledove
>   is heard in our land.
> The fig tree puts forth its figs
>   and the vines are in blossom;
>   they give forth fragrance.
> Arise, my love, my fair one,
>   and come away. (Song of Songs 2.12–14)

The Old Testament is also full of allusions to the ways in which the trees of creation are useful to humankind. Their wood was used extensively in building houses (2 Samuel 7.2), the Ark (Genesis 6.14–22), ships (Ezekiel 27.4–9) and temples (1 Kings 6.20ff.). They were also used to make household furniture and tools and objects like spinning wheels (Proverbs 31.10). Biblical history spans many generations but it appears that all the different kinds of woods and their uses were very well known to the builders, artisans and craftsmen of those times.[2]

Human beings are somewhat like those trees. Unlike them, however, people are endowed with consciousness, intelligence and free will. These qualities find expression in human language and behaviour. Human beings are always recognizable as persons, yet they differ from each other in many ways. Individuals are called by God to specific tasks, often in a unique manner. People can allow themselves to be shaped by him for his good purposes, and that is precisely what he does when he meets them in prayer.

It is, however, when people are likened to the properties of particular trees in the Bible that different aspects of their relationship with God can be seen.

The writer of Psalm 92, for instance, rejoices in the righteous whom he compares to the familiar and flourishing trees of Lebanon:

> The righteous flourish like the palm tree,
> and grow like a cedar in Lebanon.
> They are planted in the house of the Lord;
> they flourish in the courts of our God.
> In old age they still produce fruit;
>   they are always green and full of sap,
> showing that the Lord is upright;

> he is my rock, and there is no
> unrighteousness in him. (Psalm 92.12–15)

Longevity and fidelity go hand in hand for the writer of this psalm:

> But I am like a green olive tree
> in the house of God,
> I trust in the steadfast love of God
> forever and ever. (Psalm 52.8)

The message is clear: God's beauty and fruitfulness can be reflected in all who are created in his image and likeness. People are meant to live 'to the praise of his glory' (Ephesians 1.14)

Human beings are created for this purpose, yet, being mortal, they frequently fall short of the mark. The prophets thundered against those who betray the Lord. Jeremiah tells them what will happen to them:

> The Lord once called you, 'a green live tree, fair with good fruit', but with the roar of a great tempest he will set fire to it, and its branches will be consumed. The Lord of hosts, who planted you, has pronounced evil against you, because of the evil that the house of Israel and the house of Judah have done, provoking me to anger by making offerings to Baal. (Jeremiah 11.16–17)

Ezekiel compares Pharaoh, king of Egypt, to a tall cedar tree and shows how Pharaoh's arrogance has brought him and his people to destruction:

> Therefore thus says the Lord God; Because it towered high and set its top among the clouds and its heart was proud of its height, I gave it into the hand of the prince of the nations; he has dealt with it as its wickedness deserves. I have cast it out. Foreigners from the most terrible of nations have cut it down and left it. On the mountains and in all the valleys its branches have fallen, and its boughs lie broken in all the water-courses of the land; and all the peoples of the earth went away from its shade and left it.

> On its fallen trunk settle
> all the birds of the air,
> and among its boughs lodge
> all the wild animals. (Ezekiel 31.10–13)

That is an accurate picture of the kind of devastation that follows a huge gale. Anyone reading it receives a clear picture of the destruction of a majestic tree. The passage conveys truth about God's sovereignty over all nature: those who are created in the image of God are subject to God's judgement.

The New Testament writers build on these thoughts and develop them. In Matthew's Gospel, for instance, the fig tree is used as a herald of summer (Matthew 24.32), but also as a parable:

> 'Beware of false prophets, who come to you in sheep's clothing but inwardly they are ravenous wolves. You will know them by their fruits. Are grapes gathered from thorns, or figs from thistles? In the same way, every good tree bears good fruit, but the bad tree bears bad fruit. A good tree cannot bear bad fruit, nor can a bad tree bear good fruit. Every tree that does not bear good fruit is cut down and thrown into the fire. Thus you will know them by their fruits.' (Matthew 7.15–20; compare Matthew 7.33 and Luke 3.8–9)

The fig tree is also used in other ways, both as a warning and as a kind of encouragement. In Luke's Gospel, for instance, there is the parable of the fig tree that failed to bear fruit:

> 'A man had a fig tree planted in his vineyard; and he came looking for fruit on it and found none. So he said to the gardener, "See here! For three years I have come looking for fruit on this fig tree, and still I find none. Cut it down! Why should it be wasting the soil?" He replied, "Sir, let it alone for one more year, until I dig around it and put manure on it. If it bears fruit next year, well and good; but if not, you can cut it down."' (Luke 13.6–9)

Judgement is real, yet the New Testament writers sometimes balance it with wonderful images that give hope to all who hear them, images of our ingrafting into Christ.

In his great discourse on the relationship between Jesus and his disciples, John uses examples from nature that would have been familiar to his contemporaries. In his speech on the relationship between himself and his disciples Jesus uses a vine rather than a tree to make his point:

> 'I am the vine, you are the branches. Those who abide in me and I in them bear much fruit, because apart from me you can do nothing.' (John 15.5)

Jesus' message would have been easily understood. Those who heard such words would have also remembered other passages in the Hebrew Scriptures that would have reinforced his teaching.[3]

Despite these warnings the authors of the books of the Old and New Testaments are remarkably positive about the goodness of human beings and their rootedness in God.

The person who wrote the first psalm is, for instance, extolling the virtues of those who 'delight in the law of the Lord, and on his law they meditate day and night':

> They are like trees
>   planted by streams of water,
> which yield their fruit in its season,
>   and their leaves do not wither.
> In all that they do, they prosper. (Psalm 1.2–4)

People can be likened to trees thrusting their roots into water, that is, into Christ, the wellspring of their lives, but there is also a sense in which Christians are like the chestnut tree in the garden. They are created in the image and likeness of God (Genesis 1.26; 5.1). When they are baptized into Christ's death and raised with him to new life (see Romans 6.5). Christ comes to make his home in them: 'It is no longer I who live, but it is Christ who lives in me' (Galatians 2.20). As people grow in discipleship through the grace of the indwelling Holy Spirit they become more aware of the abiding presence of the Trinity in their lives; they are enclosed in the heart of the Trinity (John 17.21–23). God being in them and they in God, they can reflect that relationship in their lives, just as the tree in the quiet garden displays the image of Christ that is now held fast in the substance of the tree, and yet comes forth from it in glory.

In time, and by the grace of God, Christian disciples become rooted enough in Christ to withstand gales. They bear in themselves the marks of the indwelling Lord Jesus (Galatians 6.17). They can offer shelter and refuge to other creatures; also, they can bear good fruit (Matthew 13.31–32; Mark 4.30–32; and Luke 13.18–19).

All Christians can be with Christ as he suffers in and with creation, and as he prays ceaselessly to God as mediator for the whole creation. They become part of his prayer, yet they are not automatons. Christ does not compel; he invites his disciples to listen to him in prayer, and to join in his pleading.

How can Christians put this theological truth into practice in their lives?

Many people begin with the Lord's prayer, the prayer whose words they learn by heart when they are children or newly converted adults. At first they just say the words. Later they grow into their meaning. In time, as they grow in faith by the grace of God, its essence embeds itself in their very being.

Whenever Christians pray the Lord's prayer, they begin by

recognizing God's sovereignty and holiness. They ask that God's kingdom should come into their lives. Then they tell God that they desire that God's will should be done 'on earth, as it is in heaven'. In asking this, they are setting God's will ahead of their own desires, even if it means that what they want to happen does not come about. Those who pray know that when they ask for daily bread they are asking for what they need rather than for what they want; it will be given to them and they will receive it with thanksgiving. In asking for forgiveness they know that the measure they will receive will be in proportion to their ability to forgive others who sin against them. In asking to be kept away from temptation and delivered from evil, they know that they live under Christ's mercy and protection. They are affirming the truth that nothing can ultimately separate them from him. All petitions to God are made in Christ's name (John 14.13–14).

The Lord's prayer is the pattern for all intercessory prayer. At some stage in our lives those of us who are Christians are likely to find that we are no longer praying it by rote, but are using it as heartfelt intercession. Once that happens, we know that every time we say this prayer we have to try to be so united with Christ that what we ask for is what he desires to ask of his, and our, heavenly Creator. Every time we say it, we are brought into the presence of God, into heaven.

There is a good argument for using only the Lord's prayer for intercession. Constant repetition, however, may dull our perception of reality. This may be why the Holy Spirit sometimes prompts us to use other forms of prayer, never instead of, but as well as, the Lord's prayer, to help us to deepen our awareness of the link between heaven and earth, to help us to 'have the mind of Christ' (1 Corinthians 2.16) as we intercede.

One good way of praying for what we and others need is to use our own or other people's words. We simply ask, as a child would ask its mother or father for what it wants. We ask with our feelings, as well as with our lips. We ask, and we go on asking, as the Syrophoenician woman did when she begged Jesus for the crumbs under the table (Mark 7.24–30), or as the widow did when she met an unjust judge (Luke 18.1–8).

Some people find it helpful to bring another person to Christ in much the same way that the four friends of the paralysed man did when they made an opening in the roof of a house where Jesus was and let him down into the midst of the crowd (Mark 2.1–12). Many like to use pictures of the friends for whom they are praying: this helps to focus attention, so bringing them into the presence of Christ. Some people can see their friends in their mind's eye without any external help, but many like to use a portrait or a statue of Christ, a candle[4] or even an icon,[5] to remind themselves of his closeness. By placing their friends and enemies in Christ's presence, they know that they are being given into safe hands. Some people spend a regular time each day in this kind of intercession. Often they choose their own time, but some find it helpful to pray at times when they know others are also praying. Groups of people in Britain, for instance, pray for cancer patients at 9.00 a.m. each day.[6] Many people and groups also pray for world peace at noon each day.[7] Others rely on the Holy Spirit to bring those for whom they pray to mind when prayer is needed.

A good way of praying for people whom we do not know, but whose lives touch our own, is to use the broadcasts of the news as times for intercession. It might be thought that doing this simply floods the mind and dilutes concentration, but experience proves that this is not so. The Holy Spirit is selective: one person may feel drawn to pray for people involved in sectarian war; another is drawn to pray for abused children, another for people who are starving, another for people in prison. At different times in our own lives we may find ourselves involved with issues and people to whom we were not formerly attracted.

Another way of interceding for others, be they inanimate parts of God's creation, living parts of the earth, animals or people, is through intention. If we offer God some of our time and energy, perhaps even the whole of our day, as intercession then God will honour our desire. We do not necessarily need to formulate our desires in words or even in feelings. Everything we are and say and do during that time is taken up and used by Christ who 'always lives to make intercession' for us (Hebrews 7.25).

All Christians are called to share in Christ's healing and regenerating ministry in the world and to be ambassadors for Christ who are entrusted with the message of reconciliation (see 2 Corinthians 5.19–20). It is only possible to do that work well by being reconciled to God, united to Christ as a branch is to a fruitful vine (John 15.5–7), as an arm is to a body of which Christ is the head (1 Corinthians 12.30), as a living stone is to its cornerstone (Ephesians 2.20–22). These kinds of intercessions will be the subject of later chapters.

All these ways are good: they combine Scripture and experience in a direct way. There are times, however, when Christians come to intercession from a different perspective altogether. The Holy Spirit sometimes prompts people to start their prayer through something that is a familiar part of ordinary life. Dame Julian of Norwich, a fourteenth-century English anchoress, for instance, was shown 'a little thing, the size of a hazelnut in the palm of my hand, and it was as round as a ball'. As she gazed on it, wondering what it was, the answer came:

> 'It is all that is made.' I marvelled that it could last, for I thought it might have crumbled to nothing, it was so small. And the answer came into my mind, 'It lasts and ever shall because God loves it.' And all things have being through the love of God.
>
> In this little thing I saw three truths. The first is that God made it. The second is that God loves it. The third is that God looks after it.[8]

It is not surprising that many Christians find that holding a real hazelnut in their hands helps them to think of God's love. From there it is but a step to enclose those for whom one prays in that love.

William Shakespeare found 'tongues in trees, books in the running brooks, sermons in stones and good in everything'.[9] So, too, can many people in contemporary society. They find themselves moved to prayer by what they see and hear. William Blake saw 'a World in a Grain of Sand, and a Heaven in a Wild Flower'.[10] His use of capitals suggests that he saw God in all creation. Many nature mystics would agree with him. Some might be moved to prayer for the conservation of nature and the preservation of the planet.

One amazing example of the way in which nature helps inspiration comes from the experience of a Welsh artist and poet, David Jones. Once, when he was ill, he noticed that outside the window of the room of the nursing home in which he lay there were three trees, a pine, a fir and a chestnut. He drew them a number of times. Then, under a fair amount of pressure from his doctor, he created a superb picture of a forest of trees, three of which dominated the scene. In this painting he drew half-concealed, finely sketched allusions to the ancient world of the druids, the crucifixion of Jesus and the collapse of the Roman empire.[11] This picture has moved many people to prayer and to a deeper understanding of Christ's sacrificial love. It leads naturally to concerned prayer for those for whom Christ suffered and died.

As Christians develop in their discipleship many find that they pray because the Holy Spirit encourages them to pray, sometimes in words, but sometimes when 'we do not know how to pray as we ought, that very Spirit intercedes with sighs too deep for words' (Romans 8.26–27). Knowing that 'God who searches the heart, knows what is in the mind of the Spirit, because the Spirit intercedes for the saints according to the will of God' (Romans 8.27), prayer becomes not so much an activity as an attitude, a mode of being, a way of becoming aware of the mind of Christ and of God's actions in and through creation. It is a relationship that fosters communication between God and those who seek to find their home in God.

Those who intercede believe that God hears human prayers and responds to them. They try to open themselves to hear what God is saying. Many are moved to action by the Holy Spirit and find themselves drawn into active work such as visiting the sick, lonely, or poor people for whom they pray. Some may become active in environmental, peace and justice issues or even find themselves engaged in political life. People who are firmly rooted in Christ will not be drawn away from him by such activities, but those who are not so rooted are likely to lose their way.

Christians sometimes seem to non-Christians to be preoccupied with sin, their own and other people's, with the devil who, like a roaring lion, 'prowls around, looking for someone to devour' (1 Peter 5.8), with their failures, with their sufferings that are seen to be pointless and destructive to human happiness.

Those charges can be refuted by some, but others of us may recognize some truth in them. If that is so, we may do better to look at God's trees, thrust our roots deep into the 'spring of water, gushing up to eternal life' (John 4.14b), lift up our heads to find the sun of righteousness 'with healing in its wings' (Malachi 4.2), in the same way that the trees of creation grow upwards towards the sun. In these ways we will be doing our best to live 'to the praise of his glory' (Ephesians 1.14). It will be when we heed the words of St Paul in his letter to the Christians at Philippi that we shall grow most easily and quickly into God:

> Rejoice in the Lord always; again I will say, Rejoice. Let your gentleness be known to everyone. The Lord is near. Do not worry about anything, but in everything by prayer and supplication with thanksgiving let your requests be made known to God and the peace of God, which surpasses all understanding will guard your hearts and your minds in Christ Jesus.
>
> Finally, beloved, whatever is true, whatever is honourable, whatever is just, whatever is pure, whatever is pleasing, whatever is commendable, if there is any excellence and if there is anything worthy of praise, think about these things. Keep on doing the things that you have learned and received and heard and seen in me, and the God of peace will be with you. (Philippians 4.4b–9)

If we rejoice as St Paul encourages us to do we shall find our peace and

happiness in Christ as Joshua Smith, the eighteenth-century author of
the hymn 'Christ the Apple Tree', discovered for himself as he
contemplated the mystery of our relationships with Christ:

> The tree of life my soul hath seen,
> Laden with fruit and always green:
> The trees of nature fruitless be
> Compared with Christ the apple tree.
>
> His beauty doth all things excel:
> By faith I know, but ne'er can tell,
> The glory which I now can see
> In Jesus Christ the apple tree.
>
> For happiness I long have sought,
> And pleasure dearly I have bought:
> I missed of all; but now I see
> 'Tis found in Christ the apple tree.
>
> I'm weary with my former toil,
> Here I will sit and rest awhile:
> Under the shadow I will be,
> Of Jesus Christ the apple tree.[12]

And, sitting under the shadow of the apple tree, we shall find that,
although we are not yet whole, we are on the way to becoming more
like Jesus, more able to understand and participate in his work of
intercession as co-workers in his kingdom.

The deciduous windswept tree that reminded me of a leaning white poplar, *Populus alba*, that I had seen in Europe.

2

The white and the black poplar

DEALING WITH HUMAN EVIL THROUGH INTERCESSION

Out of the ground the Lord God made to grow every tree that is pleasant to the sight and good for food, the tree of life also in the midst of the garden, and the tree of knowledge of good and evil ... The Lord God took the man and put him in the garden of Eden to till it and keep it. The Lord God commanded the man, 'You may freely eat of every tree in the garden; but of the tree of knowledge of good and evil you shall not eat, for in the day that you eat of it you shall die'. (Genesis 2.9, 15–17)

Therefore, just as sin came into the world through one man, and death came through sin, and so death spread to all because all have sinned. (Romans 5.12)

During adolescence I was fascinated by mythology. I loved the story of Orpheus who went into Hades to rescue his wife, Eurydice. I feasted on the tale of Leuce, daughter of Oceanus whom Hades had brought to the underworld. Leuce's symbol was the white poplar. I had seen such poplars on my travels through Europe. They spoke to me of Leuce's journey through the waters of death.

Like many young people of my generation who were brought up on Greek mythology and on the Bible, I was impressed by all myths and stories that recounted journeys across the river Styx. I would gaze at a picture of the Last Judgement by Michelangelo and shiver with fear as I contemplated the dreadful sight of Christ casting the souls of sinners into hell. I was repelled by the ghastly delight on Charon's face as he bundled them into the boat that would convey them to eternal damnation.

It was just after I had become a Christian that I came across the mythical black poplars and willows that were said to flourish in the dry waters of death. I had never before thought about dry water, sterility, shrivelled-up trees, but now I remembered seeing dead trees, blackened trees, by river beds that had dried up.

'Are there two rivers', I asked myself, 'Charon's dry Styx that leads to hell and the river of water through which we have to pass on our way to heaven?'

There was no answer. When I put my dilemma to the parish priest who was teaching me about Christian life I was greeted with blank incomprehension and given John Bunyan's Pilgrim's Progress to read. I enjoyed it, particularly the part where Christian has to go through the deep river before reaching the gates of the heavenly city. It did not, however, help me to understand the Styx. Nothing did, until one day, quite suddenly, the black poplar tree merged into the white tree inside me.

It happened because I was on a road in the West of England that ran past a hill whose summit was crowned by a single deciduous tree that stood out against the skyline. The tree had a beautiful shape, and the rounded contour of the ground beneath it resembled a woman's breast. No roads led to that hill top. Anyone who wanted to reach it would have faced a steep climb before he or she reached its crest.

Many people who passed that tree probably would have admired its beauty, and thought no more about it. On that day, however, I saw it in a different way. Just before I came upon it, I had been musing on the problem of good and evil inside myself. The tree reminded me of a white poplar I had seen in France. Now, quite suddenly, I saw the images of white and black poplar trees fuse into one tree, my tree on the hill. The breathtaking beauty of the tree and its surroundings contained promises of good, and of evil. It was seductive. It invited an approach: simultaneously it forbade advance, lest arrival should uncover detail that would destroy a primal innocence that longs for paradise.

As I stood gazing at the graceful leaning tree, I suddenly realized that good and evil could coexist in one person, just as dead wood and living wood coexist in all trees that are alive. The tree had become for me a symbol of the tree of the knowledge of good and evil standing in paradise.

Insights such as this one are not uncommon among young people. Temptation, particularly sexual temptation, is at its height during late adolescence and early adult life. Many young people are frightened by their capacity for evil. Selfishness collides with concern for the welfare of others. Egotism fuels a desire for rebellion. Some young people search for experience and in the process may come to harm through the excessive use of alcohol, drugs, or the stimulus of danger. Their destructive desires war against the good dispositions that their parents tried to instil in them during their formative years. They struggle to make sense of their experience and in the process may come up with insights that are as complex as mine was.

Christians have particular difficulties with the interior war between good and evil since their ideals and behaviour are bound up with gospel imperatives such as: 'Love your enemies' (Matthew 5.44); 'Forgive "seventy seven times"' (Matthew 18.22); 'If you wish to be perfect, go, sell your possessions, and give the money to the poor, and you will have treasure in heaven; then come, follow me' (Matthew 19.21). How can one pray for a person one detests? Or for someone who will not forgive? What is the quality of one's prayer for a friend when one is consumed with jealousy because he or she has won the coveted scholarship that one wanted? How is it possible to pray for someone who has raped and killed a small child?

These, and other questions about the coexistence of good and evil, have provided the spur that has helped me to think about the way in which interaction between good and evil affects the way in which people intercede in a world that often seems captivated by evil.

No one has yet come up with a universally satisfying solution to the question about how and why moral evil came into a world created by God. Natural suffering, moral evil and sin seem to many to be incomprehensible realities. Many Christians, however, try to address the problem so that eventually they can help in God's work of overcoming evil in themselves and in the world through prayer and action.

At the outset of this exploration some people find themselves struggling with the biblical accounts of how Adam and Eve disobeyed God. After Adam and Eve ate of the forbidden fruit, 'the eyes of both were opened, and they knew that they were naked' (Genesis 3.7). As representatives of humankind they were told of the consequences of this primal disobedience:

> Then the Lord God said, 'See, the man has become like one of us, knowing good and evil; and now, he might reach out his hand, and take also from the tree of life, and eat, and live for ever' — therefore the Lord God sent him forth from the garden of Eden to till the ground from which he was taken. (Genesis 3.22–24)

Whether the biblical narrative is an illustration of actuality or a myth containing eternal truth, it still has considerable influence in some societies. Many people still believe that from the time that human beings were created, or shortly after, they have known the difference between good and evil. They can choose between the two. In the Judaeo-Christian tradition people were urged by Yahweh to 'choose life' (Deuteronomy 30.19). The Law and commandments were given to Moses to help men and women to do just that (Exodus 24.12; 34; Deuteronomy 5). In all parts of the world where the ten commandments have been held in respect, they have been the foundation stones of the laws and morals of human society.

When Christ came into the world, he completed the Law and the prophets: he taught his disciples to live according to certain principles that are enshrined in the Sermon on the Mount (Matthew 5 – 7). We are told that 'when Jesus had finished saying these things, the crowds were astounded at his teaching, for he taught them as one having authority, and not as their scribes' (Matthew 7.28–29). Christ's teaching has continued to make a deep impression on all parts of the world where it has been preached and heard by the grace of the Holy Spirit.

People who are alive today are able to distinguish between good and evil through a kind of inherited wisdom that is passed on from generation to generation through a corpus of teaching that is integral to the human society into which they are born. That inheritance comes into consciousness as they grow and develop into childhood and adulthood.

The ability to choose between good and evil may be part of human nature, but many factors combine to dispose human beings to one side or the other. Upbringing and environment matter. If children remain ignorant about what is good and what is evil because they are not taught the difference, they can hardly make an informed choice between the two. If young people are taught that good is evil and evil is good by adults who are close to them and have a strong influence in their lives, they may be surprised when they find themselves being punished for misdemeanours, sins and crimes that most people in their family, local community and society still hold to be anti-social.

Those who are alive today live in a time when the old certainties about the distinction between good and evil have disappeared. It is a time where more people live by relatives rather than by absolutes. In a pluralistic, multi-faith society there are many moral standards on offer. It is not surprising that this situation is causing people to become confused about goodness and evil, right and wrong.

In such a climate of bewilderment, individuals have to find standards that can help them to sort out the personal values that make it possible for them to live at peace with their own consciences. In infancy and early childhood an individual's knowledge of good and evil depends upon his or her parents and infant teachers. Later, peer-group standards muddy the water, and the clarity of a child's perception between right and wrong is diminished. As children grow into young people, however, they develop a personal morality of their own. Usually, it is a mixture of what they have learnt from their parents and teachers, and what they have learnt through personal experience and peer-group encounter. Church and church-related groups have their part to play in the formation of this emergent personal morality. None of these influences, however, can equal the experience of encounter with Christ, with Love incarnate. That is why many churches make considerable efforts to help people to meet and get to know Jesus.

The best way of getting to know Jesus is through meeting him in Scripture, prayer and the sacraments. People, being human, differ in their approaches to the Word of God, to worship, to the inward and invisible encounter with him through the outward and visible reality of the sacraments. Their approach, be it through the breaking open of the Word in Scripture, humble prayer in a private room (Matthew 6.7–15), charismatic worship (1 Corinthians 14.26–33), corporate prayer (Acts 1.12–14), or a service of 'the breaking of the bread' (Acts 2.42, 46; 20.7), is immaterial. What matters is their readiness for the encounter with Christ, their willingness to wait for God's timing, their response to his generosity. What matters more is the encounter itself, whether it be veiled in darkness, flooded in light, or comes through a quiet meeting with a friend or a more dramatic baptism in the spirit (Acts 2.1–13; 10.44–48).

This kind of encounter with Jesus prepares his disciples for the battle between good and evil that may take place in themselves through the struggle against temptation to sin. That battle is made harder by the fact that it is not always easy to distinguish between right and wrong, good and evil. Angels of darkness frequently masquerade as angels of light, as Satan did when he tempted Jesus in the desert and was answered by Jesus in words from Scripture (Matthew 4.1–11; Mark 1.12–13; Luke 4.1–13). Matthew tells his readers how easy it is to go down an attractive road without realizing where it is going:

'Enter through the narrow gate; for the gate is wide and the road is easy that leads to destruction, and there are many that take it. For the gate is narrow and the road is hard that leads to life, and there are few who find it.' (Matthew 7.13–14)

He follows this passage with one that warns against false prophets:

'Beware of false prophets who come to you in sheep's clothing but inwardly are ravenous wolves. You will know them by their fruits. Are grapes gathered from thorns, or figs from thistles? In the same way, every good tree bears good fruit, but the bad tree bears bad fruit. A good tree cannot bear bad fruit, nor can a bad tree bear good fruit. Every tree that does not bear good fruit is cut down and thrown into the fire. Thus you will know them by their fruits.' (Matthew 7.15–20; Luke 6.43–44)

That is true, provided you skin and cut open the fruit before you eat it. Sometimes fruit that looks perfect can conceal the maggot within.

This thought takes me back to the tree on the brow of the hill that was, and is, so seductive, yet imbued with danger; for it links what can happen in prayer with the tree of the knowledge of good and evil. Good and evil are related to each other: while time exists, they are held together within God's all-encompassing love.

There are several ways of looking at the tree on the hill. The two ways that I am going to describe are only an illustration of the way in which two conflicting images can rise to the surface of a human being's consciousness and cause difficulties during prayer. It would be perfectly possible to find several other ways of looking at that tree; not all of them would bring up gender imagery in such a troublesome way.

The tree on the brow of the hill can be seen as a representation of Christ, 'the apple tree', rooted in the good earth of creation that includes men and women whom God has created in his own image. Those who adopt that image are imbued with hope, for they see Christ coming to make his home with them, as he came into Mary (Luke 1:26–38). They see earth as God-bearing and tree as God-rising. They see earth, tree, fruit and the kingdom of God as a unity — God-abiding (John 15.1–11; 1 Peter 1.22–25; 1 John 3.9–10). They begin to see divinity and humanity united in the person of Christ. They begin to see themselves encompassed in God's love.

Simultaneously, however, it is possible to see earth, matter, woman, womb as a kind of prison, and tree, spirit, man, phallus as that which escapes from the earth and thrusts itself towards God in heaven. This separation of earth and heaven, woman and man, has in the past led to a dualism that caused Christians to fear or despise matter and exalt spirit. When women and men respectively are identified with matter and spirit, such dualism can influence people to make certain theological assumptions about the nature of women and men. So Tertullian in his famous passage speaks to women on behalf of many men:

> And do you not know that you are Eve? God's sentence hangs still over all your sex and His punishment weighs down upon you. You are the devil's gateway; you are she who first violated the forbidden tree and broke the law of God. It was you who coaxed your way around him whom the devil had not the force to attack. With what ease you shattered that image of God: man![1]

That, of course, is an extreme view and no one would openly admit to sentiments of that kind now, but it contains feelings that sometimes persist below the surface of consciousness. The identification of women with the earth and badness, and of men with heaven and goodness, runs so deep in humanity's collective unconscious that it influences some of us more than we know. Whole theologies are built upon Augustine's view of women in relation to God and men:

> The woman together with her own husband is the image of God, so that the whole substance may be one image; but when she is referred to separately in her quality of helpmate, which regards the woman herself alone, then she is not the image of God; but as regards the man alone, he is the image of God as fully and completely as when the woman too is joined with him.[2]

These kinds of attitudes may be deeply rooted in the subconscious of an individual; they may also lurk in the collective unconscious of humankind. This is an isolated example. The principle, however, remains important. Whenever two or more opposing images, ideas, beliefs or feelings preoccupy the mind and heart of anyone, that person is likely to experience conflict when they come to prayer, either alone or at a public service of worship.

This may cause great distress to Christians who take prayer seriously. They want their minds to be empty so that they may be filled with God. They come to prayer and find themselves full of unpleasant thoughts, doubts, even blasphemies against God. They try to pray for their mother and find themselves facing resentment, anger and desire for her death. They come to a Eucharist and find themselves full of resentment against their irritating neighbour. They know they should exchange the kiss of peace: instead, they find themselves wanting to withdraw behind a parapet of hostility to the whole idea of touching someone whom they either do not know well, or dislike. These simple examples could be multiplied a hundredfold in all sorts of different ways and spheres of human experience.

People are not only subject to unpleasant temptations during prayer and worship. They may fall into sin. St Paul expresses his difficulties with such temptations in his letter to the Church in Rome. After writing vividly about the way in which he sometimes feels overtaken by sin so that he does what he does not want to do he comments:

> So I find it to be a law that when I want to do what is good, evil lies close at hand. For I delight in the law of God in my inmost self, but I see in my members another law at war with the law of my mind, making me captive to the law of sin that swells in my members. (Romans 7.21–23)

He immediately goes on to recognize that God through Jesus Christ can rescue him from this bondage to sin. The next chapter in this letter to Christians in Rome is devoted to the way in which 'the law of the Spirit of life in Christ Jesus' sets us 'free from the law of sin and of death' (Romans 8.1ff.).

Many who read those words understand that human beings do not need to be dominated by human nature for they can call on the Holy Spirit to 'put to death the deeds of the body' (Romans 8.13). They feel called to share Christ's suffering (and this includes temptation), 'so that we may also be glorified with him' (Romans 8.17). They know from personal experience that 'the Spirit helps us in our weakness' (Romans 8.26). In that chapter, with its great shout of triumph at its end, Paul asks his readers 'Who will separate us from the love of Christ?' He answers:

> No, in all these things we are more than conquerors through him who loved us. For I am convinced that neither death, nor life, nor angels, nor rulers, nor things present, nor things to come, nor powers, nor height, nor depth, nor anything else in all creation, will be able to separate us from the love of God in Christ Jesus our Lord. (Romans 8.37–39)

Many of us find it difficult to put what St Paul is saying into practice. We read the chapter, but we do not easily believe it can apply to our lives. We do have faith in Christ; yet we may not be confident about our ability to rely wholly on grace. We know from personal experience of the strength of sin in our own lives. Our personal experience and wavering wills are confronted by faith. Through faith we can call on indwelling Love to cast out fear and overcome evil. God's grace is enough for us if only we claim it, 'for power is made perfect in weakness', as St Paul wrote to another church (2 Corinthians 12.9).

God knows everything about us. So we would deceive ourselves, rather than God, if we tried to bring only our good thoughts and feelings to God in prayer. Instead we can honour God by consciously bringing the whole of ourselves into our prayer. When we start trying to do this, we may find ourselves afraid of the strength of the evil that is part of us. Indeed, some of us feel consumed by evil and cannot find any good in ourselves. We may shrink from coming to God in such a condition. It is, however, precisely then that we should be coming to our Saviour for him to heal, restore and change us.

If we persist in prayer, and allow Love to overcome our fears, we will gradually find that our temptations become gifts that can be offered to God. We simply stand before God, holding out these unpleasant thoughts and feelings to Christ. Simultaneously, if we can, we call up thoughts and feelings that contradict the temptation. We can probably only do this by faith rather than by conscious recall of positive ideas and emotions. We then hold both sets of thoughts and feelings to Christ. As we do this we cleave to him by faith. We know that he will heal us from all that might harm us. We know that he wants our good.

At a practical level all that needs to be done is to wait on Christ with our gifts held out to him. We may have to wait for some time, but if we do so with steady courage we shall find that Christ does take away the desire to veer in the direction of evil. He redirects the energy that could have been used for an evil act. Instead, he uses it to plead to the Father on our and other people's behalf, and for good of his whole creation. He also uses it for his healing work in the world. We could not do that, but he can.

This task of holding two opposites enclosed within the unity of God's love is initiated by the Holy Spirit and brought to completion by him for our healing, but never for our benefit alone. God may also ask us to hold on to two opposites in this kind of creative and fruitful way in other situations. God may, for instance, call us to take hold of this kind of experience as part of our prayer of intercession.

Much intercession is straightforward pleading to God for ourselves and for others for whom we feel concern, or who have asked for our prayers because they are in some kind of trouble, dilemma, conflict or crisis. We pray with sincerity and we persevere in prayer. Our prayers do not disturb our interior peace because the problems of those for whom we pray do not resonate with our own interior difficulties, temptations and problems. There are times, however, when our pleading for others stirs up our own interior turmoil. When that happens, we may find ourselves drawn into intercession that involves interior conflict between contrasting images, thoughts and feelings in ourselves.

A saint of God who epitomizes this kind of double-sided experience in prayer is St Thérèse of Lisieux, who was afflicted with terrible temptations against faith during the last period of her life. After fifteen months of darkness and doubt she told her sister Pauline that she never 'debated with' her dark thoughts. She knew that they must be endured. She added: 'But while they are imposed upon me, I make acts of faith incessantly.'[3]

One of her biographers, Ida Friederike Görres, states Thérèse sometimes knew that her terrible doubts and the internal anguish that they caused her had to be endured because they were her way of sharing in the anguish of souls outside her convent walls. Görres says:

In hours of insight, however, she understood that this terrible and, as she so often repeated, 'incomprehensible' state was not a fault but a task, which she was required to participate in the sins of the world outside the convent walls, where violent attacks raged against the existence of the soul, against immortality and the 'hereafter'. She grasped that she was atoning not only by praying at a safe distance for those poor Godless souls, but by being right in the midst of them, sharing all their torments and their blindness, being one of them, and having to appeal to God's mercy. She was participating in the unfathomable Passion of Our Lord when His Father abandoned Him. And wholeheartedly, Thérèse committed herself to this suffering.[4]

Thérèse identified with all who are tormented by doubt. She was undoubtedly a heroic soul, a great exemplar of the 'little way' of allowing her 'small' sufferings to join her to those for whom she prayed by the grace of Christ who called her to that work. This kind of work, however, is not confined to those who are enclosed contemplative nuns. It is work which many Christians who live in the world are also called to do.

Intercessory prayer of this double-sided kind is more common among Christians than some of us think. It is relatively easy to understand what is happening if the temptations are confined to a single issue, such as doubts that God exists. It is, however, comparatively rare to experience assault by temptation on one front only. Often it comes on many fronts; too often, people fail to overcome it because they are not quick enough or single-minded enough to look only at God as St Thérèse evidently did. Although she felt she did not believe, she continued to live her faith and to write about God as if she had no doubts at all. Our struggles are often less courageous than hers. We wallow in the mire and sometimes 'go under'; yet if we rely wholly on grace, and not on our own strength, we shall find that there are moments of insight when we can know the truth of Dame Julian of Norwich's words about God's will for us:

> He did not say, 'You shall not be tempest-tossed, you shall not be work-weary, you shall not be discomforted.' But he said, 'You shall not be overcome.' God wants us to heed these words so that we shall always be strong in trust, both in sorrow and joy.[5]

God uses our human capacity for double-sided prayer when we are in situations where we can devote time to quiet prayer, but we may also find ourselves praying in this way in other circumstances. We may, for instance, find ourselves in the middle of a family or workplace conflict, and have to pray on the spot. We may not be involved directly in the conflict and yet find ourselves having to pray for long periods of time for people on different sides of a dispute about fundamental issues.

Such situations are not uncommon. During the 1939–45 world war, for instance, families sometimes found themselves on opposing sides. English women married to German men might find themselves living in Berlin, but be torn by anxiety about their relatives in London who were in constant danger from air raids. A similar situation might well occur in reverse. Christians who found themselves in such circumstances would be drawn into prayer for their relatives on both sides of the war. They might find themselves sympathizing with both sides. They might even feel themselves to be facing both ways at once, rather like the Roman god Janus, whose image the Romans placed over the gates at the entrance of their homes, fortresses and cities. The carving was always double-faced, double-sided. One face looked outwards to watch for approaching enemies: the other faced inwards to watch over and protect the residents and to encourage the emergent armies of defence and attack.

Such prayer makes great demands on the intercessors. To outsiders, praying for people on both sides of a war can seem like an abrogation of responsibility. It can look as if someone who prays in that way is 'sitting on the fence'. It can seem as if he or she were condoning evil and doing nothing to help to resolve the conflict. So, for instance, an English mother living with her German family might find herself praying for her son who is in the German army and for her brother who is in the British army. She prays for both with equal intensity. Imagine, however, that instead of being an officer in the German army at the front her son were to be put in charge of an extermination camp. Her love for him might prevent her from being able to criticize his actions as camp commandant. Her love and compassion for her brother, however, might tear her apart were she to hear of his capture and imprisonment in that same camp. How then should she pray?

The answer may seem plain: she should pray for the overthrow of the regime that is committing or condoning evil acts, even if that also means that eventually her son will be tried and may be executed as a war criminal. In reality, the answer is not so simple: for her son might be more kind, more compassionate, more just than most of his potential replacements. He might spare her brother and other internees where others might not. In this situation she might appear to be sitting on the fence, whereas in reality she had decided to pray and work for the overthrow of a regime she clearly saw as evil, while, simultaneously, she prayed for her son and her brother with equal love. That kind of intercession and/or action is very costly indeed.

What this example suggests is that while it is important to hold to a balance of sympathies in all intercession where one is praying for individuals on both sides of a conflict, it is also necessary to make choices between good and evil. It is necessary to stand firmly within God, to choose between 'life or death, blessing or curse' (Deuteronomy 30.19), 'to refuse the bad and choose the good' (Isaiah 7.15). It is only in this way and from this stance that one can hold out opposing people on different sides of a conflict to God for God to reconcile and heal through the work of Jesus on the cross.

In his book *The Powers and the Life of the Spirit*, Walter Wink points out:

> Prayer is never a private act. It may be the interior battlefield where the decisive victory is first won, before engagement in the outer world is even attempted.[6]

He also makes the point that one must take one's stance by citing the principles that underlay Gandhi's non-violent resistance:

> Gandhi insisted that we must never accept evil, even if we cannot change it. Accepting evil, no matter how monolithic, inevitable, or entrenched, serves to deaden moral sensitivity. It creates a public inertia that will in time baptize what is wrong as inevitable or necessary. Calling evil by its name — naming as evil what others regard as custom (wife beating) or natural (homophobia) or even moral (executing political critics or religious heretics) — maintains the moral nerve even in circumstances where change seems impossible.[7]

Although it is not always easy to distinguish between what is good and what is evil this principle and its consequences hold good for a number of contemporary issues in Church and society alike. Those who follow Christ are encouraged by him to care about the poor, the oppressed, the enslaved peoples of the world. At the same time they can pray with integrity for the rich, the oppressors and the slave-keepers of the world. They will do their best work for God by becoming aware of the complex issues that underlie any serious conflict, be it one of church doctrine and order, or one of social justice and peace. Such people will try to base themselves firmly on the side of God. They will allow the conflict between good and evil to surface to consciousness in prayer and then hold it out to God for his healing.

There is also a prophetic element in such intercessory prayer. There are times when Christians feel called to witness in public to their beliefs. Some may be called, for instance, to stand with those who urge politicians to impose a total ban on landmines. Knowing all the arguments that are advanced in favour of retaining these kinds of anti-personnel weapons, they nevertheless take their stand with those who oppose them. They know that they must always pray for those whose livelihood depends upon the manufacture of such weapons, for governments who believe themselves to be justified in using them, for those who are terribly maimed when they explode under them, and for their dependants. Yet their prayers still prompt them to action, to public protest, to witness. Such action may bring them considerable discomfort of the kind of which Dame Julian spoke in another context (see p. 30). Those of us who do not feel impelled by the Holy Spirit to such action have to respect them and, with them, believe that it is what God wants of them. Even if we think them wrong, we can believe that in the end, as God said to Dame Julian, 'All shall be well, and all manner of thing shall be well'.[8]

The tree on the brow of the hill may die one day, but the tree of the knowledge of good and evil will always be present in our lives until the end of time. Our lives are touched by its existence. We have choices to make. Even if we are tempted to think that by standing in the middle we probably can escape personal involvement, we know that as Christ's disciples we have already made our choice between good and evil. All we have to do is to respond to his call concerning which people and issues we will pray about and act upon.

This double-sided prayer, or Janus prayer, if one wants to use a shorthand word to describe it, can be a way of participating in Christ's intercessory, reparative and reconciling work on the cross. I have found, however, that whenever I have tried to get close enough to Calvary to contemplate his work on the cross I have been led along the path that leads past the trees of idolatry.

A hardwood tree seen in Liberia.

3

The holm tree

BY-PASSING IDOLATRY IN PRAYER

The carpenter stretches a line, marks it out with a stylus, fashions it with planes, and marks it with a compass; he makes it in human form, with human beauty, to be set up in a shrine. He cuts down cedars or chooses a holm tree or an oak and lets it grow strong among the trees of the forest. He plants a cedar and the rain nourishes it. Then it can be used as fuel. Part of it he takes and warms himself; he kindles a fire and bakes bread. Then he makes a god and worships it, makes a carved image and bows down before it. (Isaiah 44.13–15)

It happened early one morning just after the sun had risen. In that part of Africa dawn comes abruptly: one moment it is dark night; the next sees everything bathed in strong light. I was returning from the hospital compound. My patient had just died in childbirth: so had the infant. I could still hear the shrill wailing of the women as I came past the banana and grapefruit trees that lined the path between hospital and home.

I was very tired; it had been a long night. As I came into the clearing by the house, I noticed the nightwatchman over by the grove of avocado pear trees that supplied me with breakfast. I knew him well. He was a villager who had recently sent his second wife away so that he could become a Christian. It was the sacrifice that men and women had to accept when one or both of them asked for baptism: nevertheless, it always made me feel sad and a little angry.

As I greeted the old man courteously, I saw that he was whittling a piece of dark wood.

'What's it going to be?'

'Christian magic.'

'Magic?' The surprise was startled out of me.

'Magic! Yes! The priest told me to throw away the bones and teeth I used to wear round my neck for protection against the evil spirits that are always seeking to harm me. He said that the cross could protect me from all evil, from the witch doctor's spells, from the bush men who come to steal our children by night, from the curses of my second wife who left today. I buried my charms — you see I

might need them again if he's wrong — and now I'll wear this instead. If it's good magic, as the father said it was, I'll be safe. If not . . .' He shrugged.

I turned to go into the house. I was too weary to start a theological argument then. No Christian missionary would have spoken of a crucifix as magic, yet I could see how the confusion had arisen in the old man's mind. The Christian priests always made people throw away their heathen charms: then they replaced them with the image of the God who came to save and heal and protect. Small wonder that this simple action had implied that Jesus' magic was more powerful than heathen magic.

The wood for the old man's carving came from a hardwood tree. The image was African and very beautiful. The old man was a sincere and committed Christian according to his own interpretation of the teachings he had received. Despite all this, I felt uneasy. I had remembered that the hard wood of another tree, the holm oak, had frequently been used to make idols in biblical times.[1]

The next day I told the head of the mission what had happened and then tried to forget all about it, but I could not put it out of my mind altogether. 'What', I asked myself, 'was the difference between an image that pointed towards God and an idol that attracted worship to itself as a substitute for God?'

It is, of course, possible that the old man in Africa carving his hard wood simply thought of the crucifix as an image that expressed a truth about God. I may have been mistaken in thinking that his attitude towards its 'magic' went further than it should have done. Yet it is also possible that his attitude towards the crucifix implied that to him it was more than a symbol. He might have considered it more powerful than the bones and feathers that formerly had hung round his neck. It was an easy step from there to the crucifix becoming an idol, an object of worship that distracts attention from God, who alone is worthy of adoration.

I was thirty years old when this incident happened. Up to that moment, I had accepted the practices of my own type of high Anglican churchmanship without question. I knew that pictures of Christ were not portraits of him; they were representations that came from within the artist's understanding of Christ's person and nature. That did not stop me from using pictures and icons to help me to focus my worship. I was happy to see a crucifix in a church, although I knew that some Christians thought that an empty cross was more suitable since it conveyed a greater truth about Christ's resurrection. I saw priests kissing stoles before they put them on: it would not have occurred to me that there was anything idolatrous in this behaviour. Yet, it was in Africa that I first saw the dangers of using images to try to convey truths beyond themselves. It was in Africa that I began to see how idolatry could creep into prayer, even into intercession. The connection was not immediately apparent; it became so after I had turned to the Bible for help.

In the Scriptures it is obvious that the Old Testament prophets feared image-making because they understood its dangers. People who made effigies could so easily turn them into objects of adoration. Moses, for instance, knew that the God of Abraham, Isaac and Jacob, he who described himself as 'I am' (Exodus 3.14), could not be portrayed. He told the people of Israel:

> You shall not make for yourself an idol, whether in the form of anything that is in heaven above, or that is on the earth beneath, or that is in the water under the earth. You shall not bow down to them, or worship them. (Exodus 20.4–5a)

The Israelites heard these words of Moses. They tried to obey them, but they lived among peoples who thought of, and worshipped, graven images as gods. They became familiar with Canaanite fertility religions by association. These Baal worshippers cast many of their idols in metal; however, there were some that were wooden. The pole of Asherah, for instance, stood by the altar of sacrifice. It was an object of worship and the Israelites tore it down and burnt it whenever they seized the temples of Baal (2 Kings 10.26; 23.6). The Israelites clearly thought that their actions were pleasing to Yahweh (Deuteronomy 12.3). To them idols were an offence against God's law. They were thought to represent an evil force that was wholly opposed to Yahweh (Isaiah 44.18); moreover, they exuded a sense of that evil:

> The images of their gods you shall burn with fire. Do not covet the silver or the gold that is on them and take it for yourself, because you could be ensnared by it; for it is abhorrent to the Lord your God. Do not bring an abhorrent thing into your home, or you will be set apart for destruction like it. You must utterly detest and abhor it, for it is set apart for destruction. (Deuteronomy 7.25–26)

The Old Testament prophets clearly see that idols are man–made (Isaiah 2.8) and futile, but they also believe that those who follow them are deserting God. In the passage that immediately follows the one quoted at the head of this chapter, Isaiah conveys, in a few words, his scorn of those who worship idols:

> They do not know, nor do they comprehend; for their eyes are shut, so that they cannot see, and their minds as well, so that they cannot

understand. No one considers, nor is there any knowledge or discernment to say, 'Half of it I burned in the fire; I also baked bread on its coals. I roasted meat and have eaten. Now shall I make the rest of it an abomination? Shall I fall down before a block of wood?' He feeds on ashes; a deluded mind has led him astray, and he cannot save himself or say, 'Is not this thing on my right hand a fraud?' (Isaiah 44.18–20)

The Old Testament view that idolatry led people to fall away from God, as they collapsed into futility and became ensnared by evil, is continued in the New Testament, but is also extended to include idols not made with hands. The early Christians clearly recognized that idolatry was not confined to objects of wood, stone and metal. The human body itself could become an idol. In his letter to the Romans St Paul condemns those who desert God for idols and tells his audience that such apostasy produces its own consequences and punishments:

> Therefore God gave them up in the lusts of their hearts to impurity, to the degrading of their bodies among themselves, because they exchanged the truth about God for a lie and worshipped and served the creature rather than the Creator, who is blessed for ever! Amen. (Romans 1.24–25)

In some of his other letters St Paul links idolatry and sorcery to sexual sins and covetousness (1 Corinthians 5.11; Galatians 5.19–20). Sometimes he makes a clear statement about such sins:

> Be sure of this, that no fornicator or impure person, or one who is greedy (that is an idolater), has any inheritance in the kingdom of Christ and of God. (Ephesians 5.5; Colossians 3.5)

The word 'greed' includes worship of possessions, food, money, material success, status and lust after the flesh. Greed that has no reverence for the Creator or creation can also lead to the misuse of created objects and beings, and the despoliation of forests and fertile land.

St Paul's words take on extra force when they are complemented by others from St John. In the first of the three letters attributed to him, he says that a Christian who is a child of God cannot be enthralled by the Evil One although 'the whole world lies under the power of the Evil One' (1 John 5.19). Nevertheless he warns his readers: 'Little children, keep yourselves from idols' (1 John 5.21).

Human beings have not changed very much since New Testament times. They still show a tendency to prefer to worship idols rather than God. Those of us who live in the twentieth century know only too well that many people who live in affluent countries of the world now give undue worth to material goods, success, beauty, status; when those gods fail us, we become embittered. Some people even idolize others who represent success. They, and sometimes we also, turn members of the royal family, footballers, athletes, film stars, politicians, even criminals, into heroes: they are worshipped while they live up to our fantasy expectations; they are torn from their pedestals when they fail through being human.

Most Christians avoid that kind of idolization. Their idols are more subtle. Human beings take pleasure in picture language. Visual images can replace reality. It is easy, for instance, to picture God, the Father, as someone who is like our own father, or grandfather, or pastor. Anyone who comes along and disturbs that portrait of a venerable and kindly old man, who loves and protects his children, may cause great distress. Most people in the audience know that God is not exactly like their father or grandfather, but is 'beyond all parts and passions', be they male or female. A significant minority, however, feel that the disturber is destroying a precious part of religious belief.

Men and women who challenge other people's cherished ideas about the nature of God are sometimes labelled apostates. In 1963, for instance, John Robinson published an article in the *Observer*. It was a pre-publication 'flyer' to his book, *Honest to God*.[2] In it he revealed some of his own difficulties with certain images of God. There was an immediate outcry from other bishops, theologians and the 'simple' faithful who felt that their own preconceptions about God as Father were being challenged. The Church of England groaned under the impact of the subsequent controversy for several years, although most of what John Robinson said was no more than what had been accepted by academic theologians for hundreds of years. Later, the then Bishop of Durham, Dr David Jenkins, initiated widespread argument when he challenged certain widely held views about Jesus' resurrection. Debate, discussion, even arguments, between theologians and theological students, are legitimate ways of searching for truth. In a different context, however, it seemed to many people that their Christian faith was under attack.

It is not always easy to distinguish between real worship and idolatry. Some Christian leaders denounce members of other faiths because they appear to worship idols when they bring flowers and other offerings to the statues who adorn their temples and shrines. Some church leaders castigate their fellow Christians who light candles in front of statues of Christ, or the Virgin Mary, or a saint of God. Those who make these criticisms believe that the people whom they rebuke are venerating the statue rather than the reality beyond it. Those who are thus condemned might laugh at the idea that they are worshipping the statue. They are not.

Many Christians have withstood the storms of controversy that have raged around the nature of God, Father, Son and Holy Spirit. They do not fall into the error of creating God in their own image. However, it is relatively easy to make other things into idols. The following examples of what can happen are not meant to imply that such things do happen to everyone, or even to many people, for they do not. The examples, however, show just how easy it is to be led into idolatry, almost without suspecting what is happening.

Those who are prone to certain forms of idolatry may begin, for instance, by placing great value on their church building. Initially, they remember that the building is there only to point towards God. Later, they begin to give such high value to the building that they forget its ultimate purpose. If that happens they find themselves doing everything they can to maintain the building, even if the mission of the Church cries out for changes to be made. At that point they can choose between life and death. They may see their danger and get the building into perspective: equally, they may not see. Then they may turn the building into an idol: they may resist all changes to its structure and interior furnishing that might alter its appearance and threaten the image they have of it in their minds. The building has got in the way of the mission of the Church. It has become an idol.

Other people may not be worried about changes to the external or interior appearance of the church, but they focus their attention on the rituals that accompany worship. Some of them put ritual in the place of God. There is nothing wrong with ritual itself. Many people find that it enhances worship and takes them right into the heart of transcendence. If, however, ritual becomes so important that any deviation from what is customary is seen as an affront to tradition it may become an idol. Anyone who worships ritual in this way destroys its meaning and purpose.

Some people place more reliance on beautiful words than on the reality they seek to convey. They resist all changes that mean any alteration to words they learnt when they were very young. They seem to forget that the version they know is but a translation of original material in an ancient language. It contained many nuances of meaning and thought forms, all of which might be better expressed in contemporary language, if it is beautiful. Some people who feel strongly about beautiful language even refuse to go to church if it means that they have to listen to a modern translation of the Bible or the psalms. Their opting out is a diminishment, not only to themselves, but also to the local community of worshippers.

These tangible forms of idolatry are relatively easy to describe. They are understandable, for, after all, buildings, beautiful decorations, rituals and words are meant to convey the transcendent, are intended to point towards the reality that lies behind and beyond them. Each symbol I have described so far can be a vehicle for the worship of God. Symbols only become idols when people misuse them and give them more worth than they deserve. Mistakes can be corrected by seeing them through God's eyes. The Bible teaches that God wants his disciples to worship him in spirit and in truth (John 4.23–24). Jesus taught that God looks into people's hearts, not their outward forms (Matthew 15.10–20; Luke 18.9–14). In a splendid speech before the council of Areopagus, Paul tried to put idolatry to rest for all time:

'The God who made the world and everything in it, he who is Lord of heaven and earth, does not live in shrines made by human hands, nor is he served by human hands, as though he needed anything, since he himself gives to all mortals life and breath and all things. From one ancestor he made all the nations to inhabit the whole earth, and he allotted the times of their existence and the boundaries of the places where they would live, so that they would search for God and perhaps grope for him and find him — though indeed he is not far from each one of us. For "In him, we live and move and have our being"; as even some of your own poets have said,
    "For we too are his offspring."
Since we are God's offspring, we ought not to think that the deity is like gold, or silver, or stone, an image formed by the art and imagination of mortals.' (Acts 17.24–29)

Intangible forms of idolatry are sometimes less easy to discern. There are times when it seems that men and women become so preoccupied with themselves and their own desires that everything else is excluded. 'I *must* go into a convent'; 'I *must* get married this year, regardless to whom; I will *make* her fall in love with me.' These are attitudes that underlie a subtle worship of self, the worship of one's own desires. It ceases to matter whether a person has a vocation to the religious life or not. The object of love is immaterial so long as one is satisfied oneself. The other has to be subject to one's own desires.

It may take a considerable time and much unhappiness before this kind of idolatry is exposed, but when it is people are generally able to see where they have gone wrong, and many of them can change their attitudes. God will sometimes use people's base motives and transform them into gold. The nun who entered a religious community with wrong ideas, as, for instance, St Teresa of Avila did, can become the faithful servant of God, a great reformer of the Carmelite order and a saint.[3] The woman who picks up a man at the office party and gets pregnant by him may in fact find out that he is the right person for her. The man who sets out to seduce a particular young woman for a bet may find himself happily married and drawn out from his selfishness by true love.

The greatest and most hidden forms of idolatry, however, are exhibited in people who pray, especially those who are called to the work of intercession and healing. In the passage quoted above St Paul makes it abundantly clear that God is self-sufficient. God is not dependent on us: we are dependent on God:

> 'The God who made the world and everything in it, he who is Lord of heaven and earth, does not live in shrines made by human hands, nor is he served by human hands, as though he needed anything, since he himself gives to all mortals life and breath and all things.' (Acts 17.24–25)

Those words should be written on people's hearts when they start to pray for God's will to be done in creation and for other people.

Christians who take their prayer life seriously are always at risk of thinking that it is by the efforts of some people that others are saved! It is not true, of course, for only Christ can save. The petitions of intercessors are pleasing to God, but it is only through Jesus that they can have any effect. Yet, human beings do not find it easy to appreciate this fact. Those who intercede to the saints of God often behave as if they thought their favourite saint was *the* person who was going to win them favours from God. The saints themselves know better. That is what makes them saints and not puffed up people who attribute miracles to their own interventions. Unhappily, it does not take very long for lesser mortals to be seduced by temptation.

Here is a veritable thicket of small trees, brambles and brushwood that can block our way towards God. Christ alone has the power to cut his way through the forest of pride that some people have in their own strength and achievements. Christians have to know that they are totally dependent upon Christ if they are to become people who are called to bring others to him for him to repair, reconcile and make whole. That is why it is so necessary for prayer to be underpinned by good theology. Otherwise, all kinds of errors creep in.

How do such mistakes happen? In von Hügel's *Essays and Addresses*[4] we can find one answer. He cites the example of a nun who tried to rescue one of her former schoolgirls from her life as a wealthy man's mistress. She wrote to the young woman and told her that ever since she had heard of the girl's immorality she had scourged herself each day until she stood in a pool of her own blood. She would go on doing this until she received a letter from the woman telling her that the liaison had ended. Eventually the woman wrote. The nun had gained her point. Von Hügel commended the nun for her actions, but other commentators, including Iulia de Beausobre in her monograph *Creative Suffering*, have dissociated themselves from his viewpoint. De Beausobre comments:

> Von Hügel's nun ... by deliberately devising and insistently proclaiming her method of coercion, was doing her best to use the girl's affection for her to violate the freedom of the girl's will.[5]

This nun loved the girl. She prayed for her. She took her to Jesus, but she could not leave the young woman to him. Instead she took Christ's work to herself. De Beausobre comments that she had rushed the girl 'into submission to *herself*'.[6] She had deprived her friend of the opportunity to make a free decision. Christ would never force her will. He always invites us to act in tune with his love but never coerces us.

Reading von Hügel's account, with de Beausobre's comment, should not prevent readers from trying to discern what really happened. The nun may have acted from the best possible motives. She may have avoided all temptation to attribute the girl's salvation from a sinful way of life to herself. Equally, she may have thought that *her* action saved the young woman from a way of life that might eventually bring her to eternal separation from God. Her pride could have added to the thicket that prevented the young woman from seeing God's love for her in its true perspective. The girl would have been exceptional had she avoided thinking that her choice was directly influenced by her desire to stop the nun's suffering.

By way of contrast it is good to look at how St Thérèse of Lisieux acted in relation to the criminal Pranzini in June 1887. Thérèse read about Pranzini in the newspapers. He had been involved in a sensational robbery. During the crime he had brutally murdered a lady, her maid and a child. He was condemned to death for this crime. He refused to repent. He would not turn to a priest for help while he waited for execution. Thérèse feared for his soul. She prayed and later she wrote:

But though I did use every spiritual means in my power, I knew that by myself there was nothing I could do to ransom him; and so I offered for him Our Lord's infinite merits and all the treasures of the Church. Needless to say, deep down in my heart I was sure he would be reprieved, but I wanted some encouragement to go on in my search for souls, so I said very simply: 'My God, I am sure you are going to forgive this wretched Pranzini, and I have so much confidence in Your mercy that I shall go on being sure, even though he does not go to confession, or show any sign at all of being sorry; but because he is *my first sinner*, please give me just one sign to let me know.' He answered me to the letter.[7]

Here is quite a different attitude, one of utter dependency on Christ. Thérèse's share in his work was to bring Pranzini to Jesus in utter confidence and to leave him there. Her humanity is shown by her desire for a 'sign'. Many of us who read that passage are warmed by it. We realize that we too can ask for 'signs' as long as we do not expect results or allow our faith to be diminished because God does not reveal what Christ is doing to us.

Idols of all kinds have to be torn down if Christians are to take their share in Christ's work of prayer, mediation, healing, reconciliation and unification in the world. Those who take intercession seriously may choose to ask a soul-friend or spiritual companion to accompany them on their journey through the thickets of error and temptation that can prevent them from glorifying God through their work. It is often easier for such a soul-friend or companion to discern and challenge errors of thought and direction that someone is unconsciously taking. I have benefited greatly from the down-to-earth common sense and wise counsel of others, so I can recommend having another person to whom one can freely open one's thoughts, but not everyone finds this helpful. Others may prefer to rely on Scripture and prayer for guidance, and some will be helped by reading about other people's experiences.

A Nigerian Christian once wrote a prayer. It is one that can be used whenever someone becomes aware that he or she is falling into Satan's trap:

God in heaven, you have helped my life to grow like a tree. Now something has happened. Satan, like a bird, has carried in one twig of his own choosing after another. Before I knew it he had built a dwelling place and was living in it. Tonight, my Father, I am throwing out both the bird and the nest.[8]

The Holy Spirit will prompt and help God's servants and friends to throw out all their idols, all their preconceptions about their own importance, goodness and holiness. If they have the humility to know that they are helpless to do anything in their own strength, they are safe to enter upon the prayer that, through union with Christ, can avail for the healing of many. St Thérèse of Lisieux knew all about this kind of prayer. She and other saints are exemplars of their calling. This vocation, however, comes not only to the saints of God but to quite ordinary sinners.

Those who are called to this kind of intercession will find themselves being shaped by Christ into a living tree, a cross on which Christ continues to do his work of saving the world, work that will continue until the end of time when he will come again and finally release his creation from sin, sickness, suffering and death. It is time now to turn to Christ's work on the rood.

Part Two

Specific ways of intercession

An unidentified tree on a road in East Sussex — seen in winter.

4

The hanging tree of olive wood

COMPASSIONATE INTERCESSION

'The God of our ancestors raised up Jesus, whom you had killed by hanging him on a tree. God exalted him at his right hand as Leader and Saviour that he might give repentance to Israel and forgiveness of sins.' (Acts 5.30–31)

Christ redeemed us from the curse of the Law by becoming a curse for us — for it is written, 'Cursed is everyone who hangs on a tree' — in order that in Christ Jesus the blessing of Abraham might come to the Gentiles, so that we might receive the promise of the Spirit through faith. (Galatians 3.13–14)

It was winter time in England. A friend and I went out for a walk along country roads. We walked briskly because it was a cold day and the wind was fresh. I cannot recall much about our walk, or conversation, until we came upon a beautiful tree, rising proudly up to the sky. Its first branches extended out sideways to cover the dark earth: had I been a six-foot man standing on the tip of his toes, I could not have reached them. Above them there were many branches, soaring towards the light. There was something about the tree that made me uneasy.

'It's a hanging tree', my companion said. 'They used to hang criminals on that tree. Such a shame to use such a beautiful part of God's creation to bring death to a man! Or a woman, I suppose!'

I said nothing, for I had forgotten that I was in England. I had momentarily imagined a man's body swinging from a rope attached to a sturdy horizontal branch, but that glimpse from the past had been replaced by the thought, prompted by the shape of the tree, that a man could have been crucified on that tree.

I was a novice in a religious community at the time. Lent was at hand. I had been thinking about Christ's indwelling presence in his baptized disciples. I suppose that my musings contributed to what happened next, for almost immediately I 'saw' the tree and I merged into each other. The tree had become a living cross, and so had I.

My 'vision' lasted only a few seconds. Then I shook myself out of my reverie and we continued our walk without further reference to the tree.

At that time I had not read the *Dream of the Rood*.[1] Had I done so I
might have felt more serene about my sudden identification with the
living tree. I would have found comfort in the felled and cross-shaped
tree's words about itself:

> Then I saw, marching toward me,
> mankind's brave King;
>   He came to climb upon me.
>
> I dared not break or bend aside
> against God's will, though the ground itself,
> shook at my feet. Fast I stood,
> who falling could have felled them all ...
>
> I was reared up, a rood,
>   I raised the great King,
> liege lord of the heavens,
>   dared not lean from the true.
>
> They drove me through with dark nails;
>   on me are the deep wounds manifest,
> wide-mouthed hate-dents.
>   I durst not harm any of them.
> How they mocked at us both!
>   I was all moist with blood
> sprung from the Man's side
>   after he sent forth his soul.[2]

The anonymous author of the eighth-century poem, fragments of
which still exist on the Ruthwell Cross in Dumfriesshire,[3] empathized
with the cross. He felt as if he was the cross, yet knew perfectly well that
the poem was the result of a personal mystical experience. In a later
article on the poem Professor Alexander comments:

> The poet gives voice to dumb creation, a voice which expresses
> incomprehension, obedience, suffering and eventual liberation which is
> the human experience of the Crucifixion ... the scope of the poem is not
> only human: all creation worships the cross, all creation weeps for its
> Lord's death, all creation rejoices in the prospect of its end and reunion.[4]

I was unaware of this poem: nor, then, did I know that many years later,
in 1968, a team of archaeologists would discover four Jewish tombs
near Jerusalem. One of them contained the bones of a young man who
had been crucified on a cross of olive wood. The young man's name
was Jehohanan and fragments of Herodian pottery found in the tomb
indicate that he had been executed somewhere between AD 7 and AD

66.[5] Moreover, I did not immediately see the connection between a life of intercessory prayer and the hanging tree. That connection was to come later.

I did, however, know at the time that something had happened which would change my life. I knew intuitively that the beginnings of this event lay in my empathy with the boundary oak of my childhood. Later, I was to discover that the human gifts of empathy, compassion and identification with those who suffer on earth can be used by God in the prayer of intercession and healing. Those who are called to this kind of work, and those who accompany them on their journey, may be helped by understanding these gifts.

Natural empathy is a foundation gift of human life. When it is fully developed it means being able to sense and comprehend the feelings, thoughts and motives of another creature. It usually makes its first appearance, however, early in childhood when young children are learning to know themselves as distinct individuals and are learning to relate to the world into which they have been born.

Many children talk to inanimate objects as if they were alive. They invest other creatures with human qualities. Some children, for instance, can talk to a plant, a tree or an animal as if it were another human being. They give the object they are talking to a human voice, their own voice. They give it feelings, their own feelings; but gradually they come to recognize the individuality of the object or creature they are relating to.

As children grow older they often begin to feel that they can sense another creature's feelings. Some children can feel a trapped rabbit's pain as if it were their own. They know that dogs and horses are sentient beings and they react to any act of cruelty as if they were the ones who were being hurt. Through close observation and empathy they can understand the language of their pets, and of other young children, whose methods of communication may be beyond the understanding of adults, even sometimes their parents.

Most young people bring this gift of empathy into play as they relate to other children and adults. By it they are enabled to intuit what another is feeling. Some children develop an uncanny ability to sense another's feelings. They can make a parent's or teacher's life a misery because they seem to know how to wind latent feelings up into a veritable fury of emotions. Conversely, they can be immensely supportive to an adult who is worried, frightened, unhappy or even desperate.

Some children lose their intuitive insights into the feelings of others as they grow into maturity. They become egocentric and indifferent to anyone's feelings other than their own. Others develop a capacity for empathy to a high degree. This variation continues into adult life.

Adults who empathize naturally with others do not feel exactly what the others feel because an individual is only able to feel with his or her own emotions. Thus the one who empathizes with another intuits what the other is feeling through the medium of their common humanity. There is always a danger that a person may project her or his own feelings on to the other and then receive them back as if from that other. Undoubtedly, though, they can 'rejoice with others when they rejoice, and be sad with those in sorrow' (Romans 12.15).

God gives gifts to all and yet allows human beings the freedom to use or misuse these gifts. This means that empathy can be grossly misused by adults. It enables torturers to feel into the minds of their victims and add to their torture. It permits people to wreak immense psychological damage on others. It empowers people to manipulate others. It enables them to use blackmail effectively.

When, however, people choose to use their God-given talents and gifts wisely and for the benefit of other human beings, sentient creatures and the whole of creation, they can use this gift of empathy in several different ways. It is obviously useful in marriage and family relationships. It cements friendships and creative working partnerships. It is also helpful to members of all kinds of caring professions, including the clergy. As with all gifts from God, when they are well used God adds to them and expands them.

One way in which God expands the gift of empathy is by encouraging it to grow into compassion. Sympathy for another's pain or plight, together with an ability to empathize with that person, can develop into compassion. Compassion is more than pity, more than a sympathetic understanding for another's pain, more than empathy. It contains a willingness to stay by others who are suffering, to be with them in their pain, to suffer with them, sometimes on their behalf.

Compassion is at the root of all relief work in the world. It includes both the desire to ease suffering and a willingness to suffer with, or even instead of, those who suffer. Any parent who has sat by the bedside of a child in pain knows the longing to endure it instead of the youngster. It may not be possible to do so, yet it is a natural desire. It is not sado-masochistic in any way, for those who are compassionate want to alleviate distress whenever they can and by whatever means are legitimate, even if that involves a willingness to suffer instead of their child.

Sometimes the longing remains a desire, but at other times it becomes an act of loving self-sacrifice. Mothers will often go short of food to feed their children and husbands. In extreme conditions of famine in refugee camps they are often the ones who die first. Fathers will throw themselves in front of an enemy who has a gun trained on a child. They will attempt a rescue under nearly impossible conditions even if it means dying themselves. Miners will descend into a pit filled with noxious gas on behalf of their fellow human beings. Firefighters will go back into a blazing house to rescue a child, and sometimes they and the child die. These things happen every day.

Among these humane people there will be some who are ready to suffer instead of another, some who choose to die instead of another. In the concentration camps of the Second World War, for instance, men and women sometimes gave their lives away so that others could live. Such action is not the prerogative of Christians or members of other faith communities, though there will be some Christians among those who suffer in this way. One immediately thinks of Maximilian Kolbe of Auschwitz and Mother Maria of Ravensbrück in this context. Father Kolbe, a Roman Catholic priest, replaced Franciszek Gajowniczek, a distraught father who, with nine others, had been condemned to death by starvation in an underground bunker. Mother Maria gave her own food to other prisoners, inspired them by her calm heroism and by some accounts 'went voluntarily to martyrdom to help her companions to die'.[6]

These are heroic stories. They inspire many to lesser acts that are nonetheless valiant in their own context. There are compassionate people among all the refugee camps of the world, living with the poor in base communities in South America, in the hovels of South Africa and on the streets of Calcutta. They can be discovered among the alcoholics and drug addicts on skid row and living in the cardboard box communities on the streets of London and other big cities of the world. You will meet them in hospitals, retirement homes, charitable organizations and in ordinary people's houses — everywhere.

Compassionate love of the kind that has already been described in this chapter is easy to understand. It is unselfconscious; many who love in this way would not think of themselves as unusual. Certainly those who show great compassion towards others, who even lay down their lives for others, but who are not Christians, would not think of Jesus at all. They just do these things because they are human beings who care about others. Christians, however, sometimes recognize this deeper dimension of their actions and know that in helping their suffering fellow human beings they are showing love to Jesus, the Christ.

Christians show their love through prayer and practical action. Through prayer they cover Jesus' feet with their tears, accompany him on the road to the cross, carry his cross for part of the way, wipe his face, talk to him, stand by his cross, pray for him, lessen his thirst, care for his broken body. Through practical action they can stand alongside and help Christ's poor, his little ones who suffer, and in whom he suffers. Such prayer and action is sometimes accompanied by a desire to make amends to Jesus for the suffering he endured when he died on the cross, and that he still bears as he shares in the afflictions of the whole of creation today and will share until the end of time.

This kind of compassion, involving a desire to make amends, is called reparation. The word 'reparation' has two complementary meanings. It is derived from the Latin word *reparare*, meaning to repair. So it is sometimes used to describe Christ's healing and repairing work on the cross: in this sense it is closely allied to his work of reconciliation.

The word 'reparation' is also used to describe the acts of human beings who want to make amends for damage or injury done to someone, or some group, all those in whom Christ suffers unjustly in the persons of his *anawim*. The *anawim* are God's 'little ones' who are hungry, thirsty, homeless, poor, sick, imprisoned, despised and neglected. They are named in St Matthew's famous passage about the last judgement (Matthew 25.31–46). Many Christians want to make amends, want to show their love, want to do so in very practical ways. And do.

It is one particular aspect of making amends to Jesus, of wanting to assuage his suffering, which has made the word 'reparation' difficult to use in contemporary Christian conversation. That aspect concerns the difficult issue of self-inflicted pain as a way of showing love towards Jesus. Throughout Christian history some Christians have thought it right to inflict pain on themselves. Sometimes they did, and do this, as an act of penance for their own sins, or for the sins of other people, but sometimes they do it because they want to show Christ that they love him so much that they are willing to share his sufferings.

It has to be admitted that in the past some writers about the spiritual life have given undue emphasis to self-inflicted pain, asceticism, voluntary mortification as a way of showing God one's love. A wide reading of the literature of ascetic theology coupled with scrutiny of the lives of some of the greatest saints of God shows that the desire to live austerely, to share in the hardships of Christ, is a natural result of youthful enthusiasm. Many saints of God have passed through this phase of their development. Later they have discovered that passive mortification, that is, the acceptance of unavoidable suffering, can be of much greater value to God than any amount of self-inflicted pain.

There are, however, dangers in both active and passive mortification. Among them are pride in one's own ability to suffer, pleasure in suffering pain and, worst of all, the delusion that it is one's own suffering that is redemptive. This is where von Hügel's self-flagellating nun fell into error (see p. 43). This is where some past writers about reparation have implied, perhaps without meaning to, that of itself human suffering can be pleasing to God and can earn God's blessing or healing. It cannot: Christ alone can redeem.

Language is sometimes a poor vehicle for theological truth. That is why it is relatively easy to propound error. Having said that suffering of itself is not redemptive, it is also necessary to say that the gift of faith can deepen compassion to the point where compassionate persons do become able to identify with Christ in his sufferings on the cross. They can also identify with creation as it groans 'in labour pains' and eagerly waits for its consummation when Christ will return to set it free from its slavery to corruption (Romans 8.21–22). St Paul must have known much about this way of love when he wrote to the Church at Colossae:

> I am now rejoicing in my sufferings for your sake, and in my flesh I am completing what is lacking in Christ's afflictions for the sake of his body, that is the church. (Colossians 1.24)

Paul was showing empathy towards the Christians at Colossae. He was also telling them that he loved Christ so much that he was willing to share his continuing afflictions.

St Paul's faith in Christ was such that he could perceive Christ at work in his own body. At the same time he never courted suffering for its own sake. He asked God three times to remove the 'thorn in his flesh', and it was only when God would not do what he wanted that Paul realized that God's grace and power came to him in weakness (2 Corinthians 12.7–11). When he lists all the unpleasant things that happened to him because of his discipleship, Paul only speaks of unavoidable suffering and acts of love, never of self-inflicted pain (2 Corinthians 11.23–33). Throughout the body of his writings, the message that Paul is giving is that of his identification with Christ, crucified, risen, ascended and present through the Holy Spirit in the people to whom he was ministering.

This word 'identification' brings us to another aspect of human existence that is used by God for his purposes.

Identification implies a sense of oneness with another object, creature or person. One is identified with that 'other' to the point where one feels identical with that other. In this sense the word can be used to describe what sometimes happens in sexual ecstasy where there can be an intense sense of at-one-ness, of merging with the beloved to the point where one seems to lose oneself in the other. It is a kind of ecstasy that is momentary, for, as with all ecstasy, it has to give way to the reality of separateness. Such experiences are not, of course, confined to sexual union. They are to be found in a quiet room, sitting in front of the fire with a beloved partner or friend. They are to be found in the accounts of nature mystics. They are sometimes revealed by people who suddenly find themselves 'at one' with another person.

The same sense of identification can, and does, come to those who pray as they become aware of their 'at-one-ness' with God, Christ, the Holy Spirit. Anyone who reads the mystical literature of religious faiths, other than Christianity, will soon come across accounts of union with God that are existentially 'like' those described in Christian literature.

The experience of simultaneous identification with Christ, and with those with whom he suffers, is sometimes given to those who intercede.

Intercession takes place at many different levels. All Christians are familiar with the lists read out in church. Many use personal lists to help them to remember those for whom they love to pray. That faithful work should continue: it is important. When, however, Christians are given the gift of identification, by which they feel intensely 'at one' with Christ and with the persons, groups or issues for whom they are praying, God may ask them to use their gift in a particular way.

This experience of identification lays the foundation for the kind of intercession that is also a way of suffering, but it carries with it two great dangers that immediately need to be answered by theological truth. The first is the danger of over-identification with the people for whom one is praying. Intercessors are led by God to feel this 'at-one-ness' with those with whom and for whom they pray; yet they must retain the certain knowledge that they are not that other. They should remain aware of the essential 'I-ness' of each living thing or person. If intercessors try to take over another person's pain and sufferings, they may fall into the error of depriving the person they are trying to help of the essential and proper responsibility that he or she has for his or her own life. They may also deprive someone of an important chance to grow through suffering into a greater joy.

The second danger is that of over-identification with Christ. Intercessors are human beings. They are not Christ. They are not able to save the world, nor, in their own strength, are they able to remove the burdens of other people's sins and sufferings from them. Jesus is the only person who can take on to himself the full burden of empathy, compassion, identification and substitution for sin.

The story of a little-known Polish nun will suffice to illustrate both these dangers and the counteracting grace that God gave to his servant, companion and friend. Her story points to the truth that Christ *is* the only person who can redeem humankind. Yet her testimony also shows us that those who are united to him can become part of his continuing healing and redemptive work for the world.

Faustina, baptized as Helenka, was born in Głogowiec, near Łódź in Poland, on 25 August 1905. She was the third surviving daughter in a family of ten children, of whom eight survived, six daughters and two sons. Her family was poor: she received little formal education. After a period in service, including one post near Warsaw, she had earned enough money to pay her entry dowry. She joined the Congregation of the Sisters of Our Lady of Mercy in Żytnia Street, Warsaw, on 1 August 1925. She was finally professed in life vows on 1 May 1933. Sister Faustina led the life of a humble working sister. She worked as cook, as gardener, as a general helper for the rest of her life until she became too ill to do so. She died of intestinal and pulmonary tuberculosis on 5 October 1938. She was 33 years old.

Faustina's life was unremarkable except in one respect: she felt called by God to speak and write about a message she had received from God, namely that he wanted people all over the world to focus their attention on his Divine Mercy. God asked Faustina to arrange for a painting to be made of Jesus as the Fount of Mercy so that people could meditate on, and trust in, the streams of mercy that issued from his wounded side. She did so: the first one was painted by Kazimierowski in June 1934 under her direction; others have been painted since, the best known being that by Hyla, which was completed in 1943 after Faustina's death. She promulgated a devotion to the Divine Mercy that inspires its users to trust in God's mercy, and it is still widely used among Polish Catholics.

Most of what we know about Faustina's interior life comes from her extensive diaries. These show the changes in her understanding of God's mercy as she grows in intimacy with him. In 1934, for instance, she made an act of self-offering to Jesus:

> Today in union with Jesus Christ, redeemer of souls, I make a voluntary offering of myself for the conversion of sinners, especially for those souls who have lost hope in God's mercy. This offering consists in my accepting with total subjection to God's will, all the sufferings, fears and terrors with which sinners are filled. I give them all the consolations that my soul receives from my communion with God. In a word I offer everything for them, Holy Masses, Holy Communions, penances, mortifications, prayers. I do not fear the blows, blows of divine justice, because I am united with Jesus. O my God I want to make amends to You for the souls that do not trust in you.[7]

A few paragraphs later she said:

> I soon learned that it was pleasing to God, because I immediately began to experience its effects. In a moment my soul became like a stone — dried up, filled with torment and disquiet. All sorts of blasphemies and curses kept pressing on my ears. Distrust and despair invaded my heart. This is the condition of the poor people, which I have taken on myself.[8]

Sceptics could say that Sister Faustina wished to suffer and so she did suffer. There is no doubt that at that moment she was in danger of error. She was in danger of thinking that her own suffering was redemptive. She was in danger of thinking that she was so united with Christ that she was acting 'as Christ'. It must also be said, however, that some Christians, with considerable experience in accompanying people on their spiritual journeys, would be less certain that such an identification and substitution could not take place. They would note that Sister Faustina said that she was making this offering in union with Christ, not in her own name or strength. That is the clue to the possibility that she *is* part of Christ's work. What also makes Sister Faustina's experiences more credible is that she did not cling to suffering for its own sake. Three years later she was in a different place altogether:

> From today onwards, Your will, Lord is my food. Take my whole being; dispose of me as you please. Whatever Your Fatherly hand gives me, I will accept with submission, peace and joy. I fear nothing no matter in what direction You lead me; helped by Your grace I will carry out everything You demand of me ... Should you take me in my youth, be blessed; should you let me live to a ripe old age, be blessed. Should you

give me health and strength, be blessed; should you confine me to a bed of pain for my whole life, be blessed.[9]

She had come to a place where she could accept joy and suffering alike from God's hands. Just over a year later she died. Her message to the world, her emphasis on God's divine mercy and compassion, her prayers of devotion were all taken seriously by the Roman Catholic Church to which she belongs. Pope John Paul II took up the message and his interest helped the speeding up of her cause. She was beatified by the Church on 18 April 1993.

The insight with which this chapter began, namely that intercessors can be like living trees, living crosses, can be helpful in considering this kind of prayer which does bring suffering with it, which does partake of Christ's reparative work. If those who pray for God's creation think of themselves as living crosses, places where Christ does his redemptive work, they will see their task is to become the place where sinful and suffering creation meets Christ. At that place there can be an exchange between the person of Christ and creation. This exchange will include all the concerns that the intercessors have brought to him. Someone who prays in this way simply stands and waits while Christ does his healing work. Nevertheless, such a person, being a living tree, suffers wounds from the nails driven through Christ's wrists and feet into the substance of the wood on which he hangs. As the *Dream of the Rood* puts it:

> They lifted Him down from the leaden pain,
>   left me, the commanders,
> standing in a sweat of blood.
> I was all wounded with shafts.[10]

The living tree and the Lord Jesus are united to each other by the nails that pierce both. The tree suffers, but not as Jesus suffers, for the tree does not take the weight of the world's sin upon itself as Christ does. The gift of sensitivity to the pain and problems of other people brings with it necessary suffering. The gift of being the rood will mean being wounded and scarred for life.

If that were all, it would be relatively easy to do the work of intercession, but it is not all. A human being is not simply a tree. A human being is made in the image of God (Genesis 1.26) and has to attain to the likeness of God.[11] This fact leads Christ's disciples to identify with him as well as with the cross on which he was crucified. This truth was well understood by many early Fathers of the Church. It finds its fullest expression in the hesychast tradition of the Orthodox Church.[12]

'The human being is an animal who has received the vocation to
become God', said St Basil of Caesarea.[13] And St Irenaeus tells that it
was the coming of Christ that made that vocation possible: 'The Son of
God was made man so that man might become the son of God.'[14] Or as
St Gregory of Nyssa put it in a more expanded form:

> The Word, in taking flesh, was mingled with humanity, and took our
> nature within himself, so that the human being should be deified by this
> mingling with God: the stuff of our nature was entirely sanctified by
> Christ, the first fruits of creation.[15]

The words of St Paul come to mind immediately:

> I have been crucified with Christ; and it is no longer I who live, but it is
> Christ who lives in me. And the life I now live in the flesh I live by faith
> in the Son of God, who loved me and gave himself for me. (Galatians
> 2.20)

This is a theological truth. Through baptism those of us who become
Christians enter this living relationship with Christ. We are, as it were,
the living flesh of the tree on which Christ dies and that also encloses
the risen, ascended and immanent Christ. We live in eternal life. We
dwell with the living Christ who is ascended and glorified, set free by
God to complete his work in the world. We enclose him, and we are
enclosed by him. In this way we have our share in whatever he is
doing.

Relatively few of us who are Christians, however, realize that fact.
Most of us, even those who are confirmed disciples, still need to grow
into the awareness that Christ is living in us and we in him. This often
takes time. We may need 'someone to teach you again the basic
elements of the oracles of God', as the author of the letter to the
Hebrews writes (Hebrews 5.12). He also adds:

> You need milk, not solid food; for everyone who lives on milk, being
> still an infant, is unskilled in the word of righteousness. But solid food is
> for the mature, for those whose faculties have been trained by practice to
> distinguish good from evil. (Hebrews 5.12–14).

Those words give most of us the incentive to learn by continuing the
practice of listening to God in the silence of prayer. They also give us
hope that we can be 'confident of better things ... things that lead to
salvation' (Hebrews 6.9). Gradually we come to understand more about
the saving justice of God and to participate in it as the rood participates
in Christ's saving work.

The Fathers of the Church have always known this. They know that the proper destiny of a Christian is to become like God. We have already heard Irenaeus and Gregory of Nyssa on this subject, but, perhaps, Maximus the Confessor is the one who expresses this most clearly:

> The spirit that is united to God by prayer and by love acquires wisdom, goodness, power, beneficence, generosity . . . in a word that person bears the attributes of God.[16]

He goes even further:

> The creature, having by deification become God, no longer displays any energy other than the divine, so that in everything from now on there is only one energy belonging to God and to his elect, or rather, henceforward there is only God, because the whole of his being, as is proper to love, enters into the whole of the being of his elect.[17]

Here are some roots of the hesychast tradition.[18] No one would dispute that union with God is our destiny, but few can claim to have arrived this side of death.

It may be going from the sublime to the ridiculous to claim that all those who are Christian disciples are becoming 'those who have the mind of Christ' (1 Corinthians 2.20). Yet it is true. Christians do have a vocation to become like God, yet all of us still await the time when Christ will return. In the words of St John:

> Beloved, we are God's children now; what we will be has not yet been revealed. What we do know is this: when he is revealed, we will be like him, for we will see him as he is. And all who thus hope in him purify themselves, just as he is pure. (1 John 3.2–3)

John goes on to spell out how his hearers can prepare themselves for that day. They are to break with sin, to believe in the name of Christ, to live uprightly, to love their neighbours, to lay down their lives for their brothers and sisters, to share their possessions with those who are in need. If they do all those things, John tells them, and us, then:

> If our hearts do not condemn us, we have boldness before God; and we receive from him whatever we ask, because we obey his commandments and do what pleases him. (1 John 3.21–22)

The task of intercessors, then, becomes abundantly clear. They are to grow in spiritual maturity. As, by grace, they become more like Christ, so they will become more aware of Christ's indwelling presence with them, and in all creation. They will sense that they are always in

Christil.[19] The longer they are the rood on which he hangs, the more
enclosed he becomes in their living flesh, the more identified they
become with their saviour. It is this identification with Christ, and with
the tree on which he died, that enables human beings to participate in
the fruits of the deed done at Calvary (see Isaiah 53.1–5 and 1 Peter
2.21–25). In time the grace of sharing in that work, and of gradually
being transformed into Christ's substance, bestows beauty on those
who become his rood and then find themselves incorporated into his
body on the cross.

The writer of the *Dream of the Rood* sees the cross decked with glory:

> Stained and marred,
> stricken with shame, I saw the glory-tree
> shine out gaily, sheathed in yellow
> decorous gold; and gemstones made
> for their Maker's Tree a right mail-coat.[20]

This beauty shines out gaily in the lives of the great intercessors of
Christian history. Writing about St Seraphim, one of the greatest of
them, Iulia de Beausobre describes him when he was already deeply
identified with Christ's prayer for humankind:

> His years slipped by, increasingly filled with the worries and sorrows of
> other men. A complicated surface pattern spread over his inner peace.
> Like a dark and fanciful net flung over the bright globe, this pattern
> underlined, through contrast, the value of his own luminous life;
> enhanced its beauty through introducing a rainbow of colours; made it
> more vivid and moving. Most sorrows he understood deeply. But some
> he could not understand.[21]

In referring to the sorrows that St Seraphim could not understand, Iulia
de Beausobre is writing about Seraphim's inability to understand the
sorrow that people felt when his protégée, 'the child Mary', died at an
early age because, as he said,

> through God's grace and her own effort, she matured so quickly that she
> can already take her place in my Lady's train of intercessors. Constantly
> she prays for us. And how we need them, her prayers.[22]

Towards the end of the book Iulia de Beausobre comments:

> A man among men, he had already lived the full life of the blessed: the
> two-fold life where the prayer of praise is joy, the prayer of intercession is
> suffering. When they are perfectly balanced, they keep the blessed within
> the fold of human kind. For in no other kingdom are joy and suffering so
> perfectly balanced as in the kingdom of man.[23]

We are not Seraphims. He shone like a beacon. We shine as candles. Yet, being quite ordinary people, we can sense that we are also called by God to share in Christ's work in much the same way.

We bring our concerns to God. We present those for whom we are praying to Christ. They are held out to him. We know the pain that sin inflicts on Christ. We know the pain of his wounds, as the rood knows the pain. We dwell within those wounds as Christ draws those for whom we pray into himself. Our pain becomes his. He suffers with us, and with those for whom we pray.

We are gathered into this mystery. Within it we shall discover how it is that we can share in Christ's work as he takes our sins upon himself, suffers their consequences instead of us, heals us and reconciles us to God. We shall see what he is doing with awe for we are standing in a place where we are given not double vision, as in Janus prayer, but triple vision. We see the depths of sin in ourselves as we identify with sinful humankind for whom we pray; we see and experience the pain of suffering humanity that he, and we, long to alleviate; we also see and share in the pain of Christ as he repairs the damage we have done and reconciles us to God.

Fagus sylvatica. The stump of a common beech tree, seen in a churchyard.

5

The wounded sapling

RECONCILING INTERCESSION

Who has believed what we have heard?
And to whom has the arm of
    the Lord been revealed?
For he grew up before him like a young plant,
    and like a root out of dry ground;
he had no form or majesty that
    we should look at him,
    nothing in his appearance that
    we should desire him,
He was despised and rejected by others;
    a man of suffering and
    acquainted with infirmity;
and as one from whom others
    hide their faces
    he was despised and we held him
    of no account. (Isaiah 53.1–3)

He himself bore our sins in his body on the cross, so that, free from sins, we might live for righteousness; by his wounds you have been healed. (1 Peter 2.24)

I walked slowly up the churchyard path, savouring the experience. When I had been a small child I had loved to run on ahead to claim the place on the wooden bench where my mother would rest. Once she was safely settled, I would look for my friends whose mothers also brought them to this tumbledown wilderness. If they were there we would run off to play. Sometimes we played hide and seek. At other times my older companions would throw two skipping ropes over the lowest of the overhanging branches so that we could pretend that we had a swing to play on. Occasionally the skipping rope changed itself into an imaginary rope ladder by which we might climb high into the tree and fashion for ourselves a secret tree house in which to hide from the grown-ups. It had never happened, of course, but it was fun to imagine the possibilities.

For a time my mother had allowed us to play in the churchyard, but one day, when we were a little older and noisier in our fantasy play, she had rebuked us.

'This is a churchyard', she had said, 'not a playground. You'll wake the dead if you go on like this.'

I can still remember the fear I felt at that moment. What if the tombs burst open? What would the dead look like? Would they be very cross? I had run to mother.

'Let's go home', I pleaded. 'I don't want to come here again.'

The next day we went to the park.

Now, returning to the place for the first time in many years, I noticed that some of my beloved trees had vanished, including my very own special one.

'Too old', I said to my companion. 'I suppose they'd become dangerous and had to be cut down. But it's a shame. They were so beautiful. We loved them so much when we were children. I thought they'd always be here. Once, this place was my idea of paradise.'

'Look!' my friend said. 'Look here.' She had seen two tree stumps close to each other. One of the cut-down trees had refused to die. From its sides shoots had sprung up. The leaf buds were swelling. Soon it would burst into life. It would never become the tall majestic tree that it had been, but nevertheless it was alive with a recognizable beauty, one that would mark the passing of the seasons as it once had done as a mature tree.

The other had died properly. Its stump displayed some soft rotting wood on one side where the wounds had slashed through the bark and made it vulnerable to the wet earth in which it was still rooted. There were no shoots of its own to be seen, but the surface of the dead wood had cracked open. In it were growing other plants, small bushes, mushrooms, lichens, rock weeds and on its flat surface a cypress had planted itself as if it had found rich soil on which to grow.

We sat on the bench in the churchyard. Snatches of long memorized sayings and verses began to flood my mind:

> Surely he has borne our infirmities
>   and carried our diseases;
> yet we accounted him stricken,
>   struck down by God, and afflicted.
> But he was wounded for our transgressions,
>   crushed for our iniquities;
> upon him was the punishment that
>   made us whole;
>   and by his bruises we are healed. (Isaiah 53.4–5)

God made you alive together with him, when he forgave us all our trespasses, erasing the record that stood against us with its legal demands. He set this aside, nailing it to the cross. (Colossians 2.13b–14)

'As I looked at the rotting tree', I said softly, 'I saw myself drawn into the side of Christ and I was healed.' I saw the bewildered look on my companion's face and drew the conversation to a close. 'I'm just imagining', I said.

'You always did have a lively imagination.'

We got up and walked on.

Imaginative and sensitive children have no difficulty seeing the potential uses of a tree branch. They can conjure up a swing, a rope ladder, a tree house, a secret hiding place, without any trouble. Adults sometimes lose this capacity, but those who retain it to some degree find it relatively easy to associate a real object with an event that lives in their minds. Some people, like myself, have the ability to make connections between what we see and what it means to us to an unusual degree. In those of us who are right-handed the logical thinking left side of our brain gives way temporarily to the lateral thinking process of the right-hand side of our brains. Lateral thinking takes over: the associational connections take place fast; they are not immediately obvious to other people because they have a pattern that resembles the way that the knight is moved in a chess game, yet they may also jump several places ahead. We know why we have arrived at what seems to us to be an obvious conclusion, but other people are dumbfounded; they often feel we are illogical, even slightly deranged.

I probably infuriated my friend by bringing our conversation to a close without explanation. It is the kind of 'loose thinking' that can sometimes lead people to discount what a person says because it seems so irrational. In this instance I did not understand what I had said either. Later on, I thought it important enough to try to retrace the lateral thinking to see if it could be supported by logical sequential thought which would be more comprehensible.

The event of Jesus' crucifixion is of importance to all Christians, both because they feel that it really happened in the historical past and because the event has significance in their own present experience. The event is re-enacted in the Eucharist and is frequently referred to in sermons in church, but if it is to have real significance in a person's life it has to come out of church, out of sermons, into everyday life. This is where lateral thinking can be so helpful. It does not replace direct mystical vision or insights given by the Holy Spirit, but it is helpful in making sense of biblical imagery.

The moment I saw the stump of the first beech tree I knew that it was not dead. The twigs and leaves that were emerging from its severed stump were indisputably recognizable as those of a beech tree. When, however, I saw the dead stump of the second beech tree I knew it was dead because there were none of its own branches visible. To me at that moment the stump signified the reality of bodily death, Christ's and ours; the cypress was a symbol of a resurrection body.

I knew at once that I had stretched my analogy too far. It was obvious that the cypress seed that had come to lodge in the old dead beech stump was alive when it became implanted in the dead stump. Nevertheless the cypress seed was to me at that moment rather like the wheat grain of the Bible of which Jesus said:

> 'Very truly, I tell you, unless a grain of wheat falls into the earth and dies, it remains just a single grain; but if it dies, it bears much fruit.' (John 12.24)

St Paul, writing to the Church of Corinth, takes up this theme in regard to questions about the nature of the resurrection body:

> But someone will ask, 'How are the dead raised? With what kind of body do they come?' Fool! What you sow does not come to life unless it dies. And as for what you sow, you do not sow the body that is to be, but a bare seed, perhaps of wheat, or some other grain. But God gives it a body as he has chosen, and to each kind of seed its own body. (1 Corinthians 15.35–38)

The husk of the seed dies completely. The seed is no longer recognizable as a seed: it becomes a new plant, recognizable, but not the same as the seed. In the same way Jesus' resurrection body was not immediately recognizable to those who saw him after his death (John 20.11–18), but there was something about him that enabled Mary to say 'I have seen the Lord' (John 20.18) and John to say 'It is the Lord' (John 21.7). He could pass through doors (John 20.19, 26) and disappear (Luke 24.31), yet he could be recognized in the breaking of the bread (Luke 24.30–32). He could also eat fish (John 21.9–10, 13 and Luke 24.40–43).

That was one picture that came into my mind, but the other, which arrived simultaneously, came from the sight of the ravaged dead stump with its gaping wounds. At that moment I saw Christ to be 'like a young plant': he is the living tree wounded and cut down, thrown away, good for nothing, torn open, killed. The death is actual. Here there is no regeneration of the stump, nothing that is exactly patterned on the tree's original life. Yet new life in the shape of a cypress tree is born. Other creatures also come to hide themselves in the wounds of the tree.

The analogy is incomplete, of course. It cannot be stretched to encompass the whole of Christ's redemptive work on the cross. Yet the idea of Christ, the living plant, the living tree on which he died, being joined to each other by crucifixion will not disappear. It is merely a beginning point for meditation on the mystery of Christ's reconciling love.

In the previous chapter Sister Faustina's true story was recounted. It was possible to see how her prayer was joined to the healing work of Christ as he shares the undeserved sufferings of so many people in the world today. In this chapter more emphasis is laid on Christ's reconciling work, that is, on the way in which he takes upon himself the deserved sufferings of sinners.

New Testament teaching about God's desire to reconcile human beings to himself is linked to the various beliefs that were current at the different periods during which the books of the Old Testament took form. For many generations, and by many different tribes on earth, it was widely believed, and still is by many, that when Adam and Eve, the representatives of humankind, were disobedient in the garden of Eden they were expelled from paradise (Genesis 3.23). Their sin denied them access to the 'tree of life', the symbol of the gift of eternal life (Genesis 3.24). Finding themselves in this state of cut-off-ness, and faced with the reality of sin as they understood it, the Israelites sought a way back into favour with God.

The Old Testament way of describing God's desire to reconcile humankind with God's very self is to be found in biblical references to the successive covenant relationships which God established with the chosen House of Israel. The following brief résumé of some of the theological ideas that underlie the many references to God's covenant relationships with God's people in the Old and New Testaments may serve to demonstrate the close links between covenant and Christ's reconciling work on the cross.

The earliest accounts of God's covenant, those God made with Noah, Abraham and Moses, describe God's desire for his people's renewal and reconciliation. Covenant meant that God made certain stipulations about human behaviour. They should observe the covenant commandments (Genesis 6.18; 9.12–16; 17.1–14; Exodus 24). In return God made certain promises to them: for instance, people who obeyed the detailed prescriptions which God gave to Moses would find favour with God, and would be rewarded by immediate good fortune (Exodus 23.23–26).

These early biblical writers saw God's promises and demands in the light of reality. They knew that blessings do not always come immediately. Yet they believed that the covenant promises would hold good in the future. So they looked forward to the time when those promises would be fulfilled, when the Israelites would enter into the promised land (Exodus 33 – 34). As if this was not enough, they looked still further ahead. In the book of Exodus mention is made of God's promise that the covenant will continue after the entry of the Israelites into the promised land (Exodus 12.21–28). It is also possible to catch glimpses of their earliest thoughts that the covenant relationship might restore them to paradisal bliss, either within time or eternity.

In the combined Yahwistic and Elohistic descriptions of the ratification of this covenant, we read of how Moses and his companions were rewarded with a vision of the God of Israel, 'Under his feet there was something like a pavement of sapphire stone, like the very heaven for clearness' (Exodus 24.10). At that time the Israelites might have expected to die if they were given such a glimpse of God in heaven, but unexpectedly 'God did not lay his hand on the chief men of the people of Israel; also they beheld God, and they ate and drank' (Exodus 24.11). According to the Elohistic account, Moses, the favoured one, then went back into the cloud and remained with God for forty days and forty nights (Exodus 24.12–18) to receive the stone tablets of the Law. In the later Yahwistic account of the same event we are told that when Moses came down from the mountain, the skin of Moses' face was shining because he had been talking to God, so much so that the Israelites were 'afraid to come near him' (Exodus 34.29–35).

The chosen people of God broke the covenant time and again. The prophets thundered at them and reminded them of the penalties in store for those who disobeyed God. Yet God's love and mercy continued to be shown to them. Once the Israelites had chosen kings as mediators to stand between themselves and God, God established a new covenant with them, the Davidic covenant (2 Samuel 7), an extension of the Sinaitic covenant, yet one which would profoundly influence God's people and lead them to an expectation of the coming of a Messiah. This expectancy is mirrored in Psalms 2 and 110.

A few hundred years before Christ was born there was a resurgence of interest in the covenant. The prophet Jeremiah speaks strongly about the breaking of the old covenant (Jeremiah 11.10; 34.18), but he also looks forward to the time when Yahweh will make yet another new covenant with the House of Israel, 'after those days', that is when the time is right:

> I will put my law within them, and I will write it on their hearts; and I will be their God and they shall be my people. No longer will they teach

one another, or say to each other, 'Know the Lord,' for they shall all know me, from the least of them to the greatest, says the Lord; for I will forgive their iniquity and remember their sin no more. (Jeremiah 31.33b–34)

These ideas about covenant, together with the messianic expectations which they promote, form a strong link between the Old Testament and the New Testament. They pervade inter-testamental times as may be seen from the documents relating to the life of the members of the Qumran sect.[1] Their fulfilment, Christians believe, is to be found in the person of Jesus.

With the coming of Jesus, God's covenant promises are fulfilled. Jesus is the new Adam, the Messiah, the eternal high priest of the order of Melchizedek (Psalm 110.4; Hebrews 5.6), the paschal lamb which must be slaughtered with Passover and eaten by his disciples (Mark 14.22–25; 1 Corinthians 11.23–25). Through his sacrifice on the cross Jesus removes the curses of the Sinaitic covenant (see Exodus 32.26– 28) by taking upon himself the curses of the Law in order to free humankind from the penalties of sin (Galatians 3.10–13). He becomes the source of eternal salvation (Hebrews 5.10; 6.17–20).

Once Christ had come, once he had been sacrificed as the paschal lamb, once God had demonstrated Christ's lordship over death through his resurrection and ascension, some members of the House of Israel must have thought that the messianic age was literally upon them. The fact that sin and death still prevailed among Christians, and that Christ's second coming, which was eagerly awaited in their lifetimes, was delayed, caused a good deal of heartache. St Paul and other New Testament writers address both the heartache, and the practical personal problems caused by the delay in the parousia, in their own inimitable ways, and the Church continues to do so even today.

St Paul faces the problem of sin boldly. He knows that, left to themselves, human beings have the potential to be the enemies of God (Romans 5.10; Colossians 1.19ff.), and of each other. He also knows the remedy:

For in him all the fullness of God was pleased to dwell, and through him God was pleased to reconcile to himself all things, whether on earth or in heaven, by making peace through the blood of his cross.

And you who were once estranged and hostile in mind, doing evil deeds, he has now reconciled in his fleshly body through death, so as to present you holy and blameless and irreproachable before him — provided that you continue securely established and steadfast in the faith, without shifting from the hope promised by the gospel that you heard, which has been proclaimed to every creature under heaven. I, Paul, became a servant of this gospel. (Colossians 1.19–23)

St Paul recognizes the fact that mortals will go on sinning even after they have been converted and baptized, but he bases the remedy for sin on faith and hope, not on good behaviour. We cannot earn our redemption. It is a free gift, given to us 'while we were enemies' (Romans 5.10).

It is, moreover, a gift that is given to all who will receive it. As soon as they turn and come within the orbit of God's mercy they begin to be made whole by God's grace. As they are drawn by God into union with the three persons of the Trinity so they begin to see that God is reconciling all creation to himself. They begin to see that when they are reunited with God they will also be drawn to live in harmony with all creation, including everyone else. That goal seems very far off, but again St Paul tackles the problem head on. Those who have been redeemed by Christ are brought into the new covenant, the 'new creation', Christ's body. There they will find others, and there too they will be given the task of being ambassadors for Christ (2 Corinthians 5.20) who, by the quality of their lives of faith, enable those who are 'still far off' (Luke 15.20; Ephesians 2.13) to experience Christ's love for them, a love that is so attractive that it draws them into himself.

So the task of the Church, the Body of Christ, is very plain. It is to encourage people to find their reconciliation with God through Christ. Once they have found their peace in Christ (Ephesians 2.14), they will find themselves alongside their natural enemies where Christ 'has broken down the dividing wall, that is the hostility between' them (Ephesians 2.11–18). Providing that they receive God's gifts of faith and hope and love they will each see each other from within Christ. Each will have 'access in one Spirit to the Father' (Ephesians 2.18). Being knit together in him they will grow into a holy temple in the Lord and find that they 'are built together in the Spirit into a dwelling place for God' (Ephesians 2.22).

Once human beings have grasped the wonderful way in which God is continually offering them the free gift of reconciliation, continually longing for all people to come near enough to be drawn into Christ's redeeming love, they can begin to participate in the mystery of Christ's continuing work in the world. This he accomplishes through his disciples.

As people grow in experience and wisdom they often find that their apparently settled patterns of thought, their understanding of events and symbols, must give way to new insights given by God. So, for instance, it is possible to see the development of these changes in perception in my own life as portrayed in the stories which head each chapter of this book. As a child standing by an oak tree, I simply saw the tree as my friend. In adolescence I became aware of Christ's presence in my life through baptism. When, shortly after my conversion, I saw the tree of the knowledge of good and evil, I was given grace to choose to live by faith. Passing by the tree of idolatry, I came to the hanging tree and saw myself as the living cross on which Christ could continue his work of healing. At that point I could have stopped, either out of false humility, or because I was conditioned to think of women as less able to identify with Christ than men. It was, in fact, that dislocating insight by the cut-down dead stump of the beech tree in the churchyard that brought about a profound change in my attitude. As I saw myself drawn into the wounded tree, and by analogy healed in and by Christ's wounds, I also saw those wounds as a place of reconciliation, a refuge for a host of creatures who could live in harmony with each other. Simultaneously, I saw that incorporation into Christ's wounded but risen and ascended body meant becoming an ambassador for reconciliation.

Although there *is* a certain progression in people's understanding of Christ's reconciling work as they grow older, the story that runs through this book does not necessarily relate to physical age at all. It is, rather, a story about progression in experience. Experience of a relationship with God can draw a person into God's work. That participation cannot be earned: it is a gift from God.

One way in which that gift shows itself to the world is through a person's mystical union with Christ. Such a person becomes so like God that he or she reflects God in all his or her relationships. We see Christ manifest, as it were, in the persons of people like St Seraphim of Sarov or St Thérèse of Lisieux. God may give the experience of union to someone who is very young as he did to St Thérèse of Lisieux who died when she was only 24 years old. He may give the experience at a young age, but delay its full manifestation until old age, as he did when Seraphim came out of his enclosure to roam freely. Of him Iulia de Beausobre wrote:

> He would have gladly returned to his former solitude, and entirely devoted the remaining days of his life to prayer: to the Godward prayer of praise and joy, and the manward prayer of intercession for the living, dying, and dead. But even more than prayer, the living demanded

guidance. This, few of them were sensitive enough to receive otherwise than by word of mouth, and, while still alive, he could not bring himself to refuse them his word of counsel.[2]

Age does not matter. Circumstance is immaterial. Saints are born into the most unlikely environments. They are made by God. All that matters is that God uses them as ambassadors.

Some of these people actually sense what is happening to them. Isaac of Nineveh, for instance, describes it as a kind of madness:

> God's love is by its nature warmth. When it lights on someone without any limit, it plunges the soul into ecstasy. That is why the heart of one who has felt it cannot bear to be deprived of it. But he gradually undergoes a strange alteration in proportion to the love that enters him. These are the signs of that love: his face becomes inflamed with joy and his body is filled with warmth. Fear and shame desert him as if he had gone outside himself ... is like a lunatic; a terrible death is a joy to him ... he no longer has his normal awareness or his natural sight.[3]

If we all had to wait for that to happen to us before we could share in Christ's reconciling work we should perhaps despair; even more so, if we listen to Maximus the Confessor:

> The creature, having by deification become God, no longer displays any energy other than the divine, so that in everything from now on there is only one energy belonging to God and his elect, or rather, henceforward there is only God, because the whole of his being, as is proper to love, enters into the whole of the being of the elect.[4]

Others have no idea at all that they are being transfigured by the person of Christ. They continue to regard themselves as abject sinners. Nevertheless they do God's work. Writing about this phenomenon of people who begin to show forth their resurrection bodies while they are still alive, Olivier Clément quotes Maximus the Confessor to show how they anticipate Christ's second coming: 'The Word comes to dwell in the saints by imprinting on them in advance, in a mystery, the form of his future advent, as an icon.'[5] Clément comments: 'The saints are seeds of resurrection. Only they can steer the blind sufferings of history towards resurrection.'[6] While it is true that the saints of God who have entered upon a permanent state of union with God do partake in God's deity, do present us with God's image, do bring people into the peace of God that is reconciling, it is also true that it is a fallacy to suppose that no one else can join in this work.

Those who are not yet saints, who are nevertheless 'called to be saints' (Romans 1.7) in the Pauline sense, that is those who belong to the household of God, are united to Christ through baptism. By virtue of that fact, they participate in Christ's reconciling work in various ways. In his second letter to the Christians at Corinth, for instance, St Paul gave Christ's disciples some very clear directions as to what they should do to assist God in this work of reconciliation as 'ambassadors of Christ' (2 Corinthians 5.16 – 6.18). He also told them how to call upon baptismal grace and carry it out. Paul's wisdom is still valid today. His editorial 'we' applies to us who hear his words today.

Personal reconciliation with God is of utmost importance to those called to become Christ's ambassadors, emissaries of reconciliation, as St Paul tells us. All sorts of internal frictions and arguments go on inside any human being. We will never be of use to anyone else unless we first understand our own frailties and inadequacies and selfish attitudes and have the humility to acknowledge them to God. 'Make peace within yourself', said St Seraphim of Sarov, 'and a thousand will find their peace around you.'[7] That is true. We shall normally seek to know that peace with God through confession of sin, either through interior personal dialogue with God, or through the formal liturgy and sacraments of the Church.

To those called to share in Christ's work of reconciliation, confession of sin involves profound acceptance of one's own sin: at the same time it is a way of identifying with other people's sins. Adrienne von Speyr, writing about sacramental confession as celebrated by nuns and monks, speaks of ways in which they may be called to share in the world's sin and to repent on behalf of others. They are in a sense substitutes in rather the same way that Maximilian Kolbe was a substitute for a man who was condemned to die (see p. 53). She comments:

> Real Christian substitution makes no distinction between what is mine and what is yours; it is rather the acceptance of yours into mine so that in essentials yours can no longer be distinguished from mine. This does not exclude the fact that the 'religious' stands at the point from which the rich young man has gone away (Mt 19:16–22) and that he thus can make some distinction between himself and that young man; but in the next instance he can still recognise himself in the person who has failed.[8]

Such work is not confined to monks and nuns. At every Eucharist, or service of Holy Communion, Christians make formal confession of their own sins: in saying '*we* have sinned' and '*we* are truly sorry' they are acknowledging that they are also confessing for others in a world where many of those others lack the ability to be penitent for their sins. They are accepting the commonality of sin and their common membership of the human family.

This awareness of the way in which human beings are linked to each other through sin and through grace is often highly developed in Christians who are called to intercede with God for their fellow human beings. They may become aware of being called to absorb some of the sins of humankind that enter their lives through prayer. They sometimes feel themselves to be rather like the old 'sin-eaters' of medieval times. These despised but useful people came out of their hiding places in the dark forest to touch the bodies of the dead, to remove from them the vestiges of sin that lurk there and to 'eat' these so that the souls of the dead could go free to God. According to the tradition these sin-eaters then returned to the dark forest there to 'become ugly with sin' like a scapegoat.[9]

Christians are not sin-eaters in this shameful way, but their union with Christ through baptism gives them a way of dealing with the evil consequences of sin that they absorb in prayer. When they become silted up with sin, their own and other people's, they become aware that they need contact with Christ, either directly, or through the sacrament of reconciliation, so that they can, as it were, re-enact the fact that God has already forgiven and cleansed them. In receiving assurance of their reconciliation with God they also share its grace with those for whom they pray in this way.

The sacrament of reconciliation, that is, confession of sin to God in the presence of a priest or other minister of God, is normally recommended when someone in grave sin seeks God's forgiveness and also *needs* to be assured that he or she is reconciled to God through Christ's self-offering love. Such a confession is also a way of saying sorry to those whom one has injured, for the minister of the sacrament represents both God and the people against whom one has sinned.

This sacrament, however, can also be used by those whose sins are less grievous, less damaging to their relationship with God. These so-called 'confessions of devotion' are not just a pious way of self-discipline and mortification. Christians who pray, especially those who are of a contemplative disposition, or who intercede for others, often seek the healing sacraments of the Church, the sacrament of reconciliation and the sacrament of holy unction, to ask for God's assured grace. By this means of loving discipline they ask to be cleansed from sins that hinder them from becoming clear channels of God's grace through prayer. The rite of reconciliation in the Roman Catholic Church, and in some Anglican churches, includes the priest stretching out his hands over the penitent's head to signify the healing action of the sacramental grace which is bestowed through absolution. It may also include an act of anointing with oil. In this way a repentant sinner is sealed into Christ's love and helped to become a reservoir of Christ's healing love which will be poured out on others.

Such personal rites of reconciliation are scriptural in origin. God is the source of all healing. The ministers who pray, hear confessions and lay hands on the sick are simply interceding and re-enacting the customs of the early Church as found in the letter of James:

> Are any among you sick? They should call for the elders of the church and have them pray over them, anointing them with oil in the name of the Lord. The prayer of faith will save the sick, and the Lord will raise them up; and anyone who has committed sins will be forgiven. Therefore, confess your sins to one another, and pray for one another so that you may be healed. The prayer of the righteous is powerful and effective. (James 5.16)

Some Christians, however, never feel comfortable with the idea of a human intermediary between themselves and God. Formal confession of sin in the presence of another person is not for them. Many of them are, however, happy to take part in healing services.

Sacramental healing services, which include the laying on of hands and anointing with oil, are growing in popularity in all churches. It is a way of asking for healing for oneself, but also on occasion for other people. Such services may be held during a service of Holy Communion, either as part of the intercessions, or immediately after the reception of Holy Communion, in itself an act which brings healing to whoever receives. They may also be held at times when Holy Communion is not celebrated.

When such healing services are held they normally include an act of penitence and general confession of sin, absolution, the laying on of hands, which is always accompanied by prayer, and an act of anointing with oil, usually on the forehead but sometimes on the hands as well. In many churches lay people will assist the priest, or recognized minister of religion, at the laying on of hands, though the sacramental act is often reserved to the presiding minister. There is a lot of variation, which merely goes to show that human beings are unique and that a variety of different religious rites and practices is needed to suit different people.

So much for the established liturgical rites: they help people to feel assured of God's reconciling love through Christ. They help people to develop confidence in and reliance on Christ. Such rites are not essential to salvation. Many people never make a sacramental confession, nor do they attend healing services: yet, through their faithfulness to intercessory prayer they are abundantly used by God as God's ambassadors of reconciliation.

Perseverance in prayer for reconciliation, providing that it relies wholly on Christ's reconciling intercession, and is supported by personal confidence in Christ, effects changes in one's behaviour. In his second letter to the Christians in Corinth, St Paul tells his readers that once they have accepted God's saving love, they, and we, are to prove ourselves to be God's authentic servants 'through great endurance, in afflictions, hardships, calamities, beatings, imprisonments, riots, labours, sleepless nights, hunger' (2 Corinthians 6.5–6). Few of us will ever have to encounter those kinds of difficulties in our personal lives, but many of us will be drawn into the world's sufferings if we are faithful to the prayer of intercession.

In this way of perseverance we can echo some of St Paul's other words to the Christians at Colossae:

> I am now rejoicing in my sufferings for your sake, and in my flesh I am completing what is lacking in Christ's afflictions for the sake of his body, that is, the church. I became its servant according to God's commission that was given to me for you, to make the word of God fully known, the mystery that has been hidden throughout the ages and generations but has now been revealed to his saints. (Colossians 1.24–26)

It is through our identification with God's suffering world, God's creatures and God's suffering peoples that we come to know how necessary it is that our prayer, our perseverance and our courage in darkness should be given to God through Christ. Whenever we prove ourselves 'through great endurance' and give him the energy of our love God will transform this energy and make it available to support and sustain those in the Body who are enduring persecution, torture, starvation, exhaustion, physical degradation. When he was in prison in

South Africa Gonville Ffrench-Beytagh experienced this feeling of being supported by the prayers of millions of people.[10] Terry Waite has also spoken about the sense of support he felt during his five years' imprisonment as a hostage in the Lebanon.[11]

St Paul tells us how we are to behave under attack, either by physical assault or during prayer: 'by purity, knowledge, patience, kindness, holiness of spirit, genuine love, truthful speech and the power of God; with the weapons of righteousness for the right hand and for the left' (2 Corinthians 6.6–7). If we keep our eyes always on Jesus and try to behave as we think he would, we shall accomplish this 'in honour and dishonour, in ill repute and good repute' (2 Corinthians 6.8), and we shall be able to enjoy the fruits of the victory that he wins for us.

It is the task of intercessors who are drawn by Christ into prayer for the world to enter into the sufferings of creation, to see them with clear eyes and hearts, to be penitent for their own sins and those of the whole world, to offer their persevering love to Jesus in the knowledge that he will reconcile them and all whom they bring to him in prayer to God. It all sounds rather grand; but in essence it is very simple. The truths that St Paul is talking about in this famous passage from his second letter to the Corinthians are captured in a vivid way by the poet Elizabeth Jennings:

> Our world is full
> Of dying Christs — the starved, the sick, the poor,
> God sleeps in cardboard boxes, has no meal.
> We are his torturers
>
> Each time we fail in generosity,
> Abuse a child or will not give our love.
> Christ lets us use our fatal liberty
> Against himself. But now and then one move
> Of selflessness sets free
>
> The whole of mankind whom he saw at play
> And work as he hung dying, when his side
> Was pierced. That spear was how we fail to say
> We love someone, but each time tears are dried
> It's Resurrection Day.[12]

Through this kind of prayer those who intercede share in the pain of the world, participate in the political wrangling of the world, and have their part in God's work of bringing peace and justice to the world. Whenever and wherever there is war of any kind in the world there will be people praying, loving, longing for peace with justice. They offer the

energy of their love to God through Christ so that it can be gathered
into his overwhelming love for the world that he has created. Through
their prayer they help God to create a climate in which peace becomes a
possibility.

Such work requires great perseverance, but it is God's work, and at
this time in the world's history it seems that God is asking more and
more people to do it. Some of these men and women are to be found in
enclosed monasteries and convents where they aim to devote their
whole time to prayer and live in ways that support them in their task.
Many more, however, are to be found among those who live and work
outside monastic houses, both in apostolic religious congregations and
in ordinary homes. Those of us who feel rather inadequate as
intercessors can take heart from some words of a great Christian
woman who herself broke new ground when she formed her
congregation of the Little Sisters of Jesus in 1939:

> Contemplatives in the midst of the world, daring to assert that their
> contemplative life can be lived to the full in crowded cities or on the
> highways just as well as in the silence of the cloister — that is
> disconcerting to those who think it only possible within a structured,
> recollected monastic environment. This is because they haven't taken
> long enough to look at Jesus, the greatest contemplative of all — Jesus
> during his hidden life in Bethlehem and Nazareth, Jesus during his
> public ministry, Jesus who only retires to the desert for forty days, far
> from the crowds, while he lives thirty three years among his people,
> simply as one of them.[13]

In Sister Magdeleine's day this was a novel idea. Mother Teresa of
Calcutta, Père Voillaume of the Little Brothers of Jesus and she all
insisted on rooting their new congregations in contemplative prayer. As
Little Sister Magdeleine wrote:

> Contemplative life is a life of friendship with the person, Jesus. It is a
> much deeper interior life, really in relationship with God. Why can't this
> friendship and relationship co-exist with a call to be with people, even
> with crowded masses of people? Is it not rather in the degree to which
> our intimate friendship with Jesus grows strong and deep that we will
> long to carry him into the midst of the crowds, to let him shine out from
> us, to make him loved?[14]

In her own time these ideas of Little Sister Magdeleine were greeted
with scepticism by some of the hierarchy in the Roman Catholic
Church to which she belonged. Now it is widely accepted that the
contemplative religious life needs an apostolic dimension and that the

apostolic life needs to be rooted in contemplation. Despite these changes it is still quite usual for Christians who do not belong to monastic or apostolic religious orders to feel that their prayers are not as effective as those of priests, monks and nuns. That is not so.

All that is needed for this kind of intercession which participates in Christ's redeeming work, is a disposition to 'pray without ceasing' (1 Thessalonians 5.18), a willingness to seek that relationship with Christ at all times, and the resolution to implore God for the gift of a compassionate heart. Such a heart can gaze steadily on great suffering and find Jesus at the heart of it, faithfully reconciling sinners to God and healing the wounds of those who suffer.

Such people are to be found everywhere in the world. Many will never be recognized as co-workers with Christ. The quality of their lives is hidden from most people, though not from all. Those who work with very elderly and sick people, for instance, will recognize the value of some of these ill and infirm Christians whose restricted lives know no boundaries. Their spirits soar free through prayer and costly intercession. Often they have dropped out of sight: they have been 'lost' by their former church congregations who may have forgotten that they exist, but the sick and elderly have not forgotten them. They are there, praying and praying. They are a hidden leaven of prayer and love in our world. They surely deserve more honour and care than many of us seem to give them.

The prayer, more than any other, that seems to be associated with this way of prayer is the *Anima Christi*. Its somewhat extravagant language may be rather off-putting to our modern ears, and for this reason it is sometimes easier to say it in Latin or in less modern English, but it is precisely that steady enthusiasm that God can use:

> Soul of Christ sanctify me,
> Body of Christ save me,
> Blood of Christ inebriate me,
> Water from the side of Christ wash me,
> Passion of Christ strengthen me,
> O good Jesu hear me.
> Within thy wounds hide me,
> Suffer me not to be separated from thee,
> From the malicious enemy defend me,
> In the hour of my death call me
> and bid me come to thee,
> That with all thy saints I may praise thee,
> Now and forever.

Those who are drawn by God into intercession of this kind, be they contemplatives in monasteries and hermitages, Christians living mundane lives, or Christians living heroic lives within imprisoned circumstances, often become the kind of people who are sought out by others to help actively in the task of reconciling human beings to each other.

True reconciliation between human beings cannot take place unless they are severally reconciled to God. Nevertheless they can come as near to that state of harmony as possible by seeking to make peace with each other in ways which do justice to all sides in any conflict of interest. We all see the cost of that kind of work every day whenever we watch the news on television or hear it on radio. We see men and women of integrity struggling for days, weeks, months, years — however long it takes — to bring those who are at war with each other around the negotiating table. Once they are there, they have to be encouraged to stay there to seek peace with justice. Negotiations often break down. When a truce is agreed or a treaty is signed the world often holds its breath to see if the peace will hold. What is happening in the public arenas of the world is a reflection of what is happening in countless homes, workplaces, communities and churches everywhere. Personal counsellors, intermediaries, mediators are all in demand.

There is a sense in which those who are Christians and who act as counsellors, 'go-betweens' or negotiators are always seeking to bring those in conflict with each other into the presence of Christ, whether or not he is named as such, whether or not the Holy Spirit is recognized as present in the whole situation. Christians who are called to this kind of active role will know the cost of such work.

To begin with they are not immune from conflict themselves. Internal tension can affect a would-be reconciler's attitudes, advice and way of working. No counsellor is immune from these human weaknesses, but those called to such work can seek training that helps them to tease out their own problems and take them into account in their dealings with other people. Secondly, in such work the qualities that St Paul spoke about in his second letter to the Christians in Corinth are necessary. It needs endeavour to discern the leading of the Holy Spirit and to go with him. It is work that cannot be done in one's own strength but only by the grace of God, only, a Christian would say, through the suffering and death of Jesus.

The contemplation of Christ's work on the cross leads to profound thankfulness. I can still remember the feelings that welled up as I stood by the wounded and dead tree in a churchyard that had become home to new life. In seeing myself drawn into the side of Christ and healed through his wounds I also saw myself mysteriously united with Christ, the broken, felled and truly dead tree, now teeming with new and eternal life. I saw the continuity of manger, olive groves and cruel cross. I saw with my mind's eye David Jones' great visionary picture, *Vexilla regis*.[15] I also recalled a poem written by a friend that spoke of that stump:

> In the garden's darkness impassive trees
> Stand sentinel, no gentle oil
> Will distil from these olives on the soil
> Where the huddled God couches upon his knees.
>
> You, O unyielding trees, you once were gods
> Asherim, held in universal awe,
> Yet here no recognition, no branch nods
> In salutation of the newest law.
>
> That like a broken stump this God should kneel
> Bent before ancient gods who priestlike stand
> Accepting this their due in a broken land
> Which only surgery of his death can heal.[16]

'Like a broken stump' Christ kneels, and yet the cypress tree has come from that stump. It is the sign of his rising and ours, the sign of the tree of life whose leaves are for the healing of the nations.

Punica granatum. The pomegranate tree, seen in Rome.

6

The pomegranate tree and the vine

PRAYING FOR UNITY

Then the Lord God said, 'See, the man has become like one of us, knowing good and evil; and now he might reach out his hand and take also from the tree of life, and eat, and live forever' — therefore the Lord God sent him forth from the garden of Eden, to till the ground from which he was taken. He drove out the man; and at the east of the garden of Eden he placed the cherubim, and a sword flaming and turning to guard the way to the tree of life. (Genesis 3.22–24)

Then the angel showed me the river of the water of life, bright as crystal, flowing from the throne of God and of the Lamb through the middle of the street of the city. On either side of the river is the tree of life with its twelve kinds of fruit, producing its fruit each month; and the leaves of the tree are for the healing of the nations. (Revelation 22.1–2)

The gate of the church which covered the site of the catacombs was firmly locked. We had arrived too early. It would be a full hour before we could enter. Struggling with weariness and disappointment, for this was our second abortive attempt at a visit, and both journeys had been long and tedious, my friend and I turned aside and walked down the steep, narrow street to find a resting place. There was none, but as we went we saw a garden centre and turned in to spend a few minutes wandering idly among lush semi-tropical plants, lemon and orange trees and verdant palms.

'Isn't it beautiful?' my friend said, pointing to a small fruit-laden lemon tree.

'Yes.' I had scarcely noticed, being somewhat preoccupied with other thoughts. I kicked a small stone along the ground, just as I had done as a small child and sauntered up to it for another kick. As I lifted my eyes to see where it had gone I saw the pomegranate tree ahead of us, half concealed by several other plants for sale.

I had never before seen such a tree. All I had seen were its fruits at the greengrocers in my own country. Once I had bought one, broken it open and tasted its seed-laden pink flesh. I had not liked the feel of the seeds in my mouth, nor the slippery feel of the surrounding pulp. Here, however, was a small contained tree laden with reddish bronze fruit, one of which had split to reveal its ebullient contents. The sight of its beauty against the rich background of other

*plants and trees, the whole scene stippled by the interplay of shade and sun, made
me catch my breath.*

*'Remember this moment', I said inside myself. 'Here is the tree whose very
life, so the ancient myths say, came from the blood of Attis, Cybele's son. Here is
the tree sacred to Persephone who tasted death for she ate of its seeds in Hades and
was condemned to remain there for part of each year. Each spring when the sun
warmed the earth she returned from death's kingdom to her mother Demeter. For
the ancients the tree was the sign of their hope of immortality. Astringent
medicines were made from its red flowers, a refreshing drink from its juice.'*

*The ancient myths about it persisted into Old Testament times. The wood
from pomegranate trees was used by Israelites to spit-roast their paschal lambs.
Their fruit was taken into the sacred precincts of the temple. The Israelites
decorated the lower hem of their high priest's robes with golden bells and
pomegranates. The bells were there to drive off the demons and the pomegranates
to remind Yahweh of their hope. As the author of a passage in the book of Exodus
says of the tinkling bells on the skirt of that robe,*

> Aaron shall wear it when he ministers, and its sound will be heard when
> he goes up into the holy place before the Lord, and when he comes out,
> so that he may not die. (Exodus 28.33)

*When Solomon built his palace he decorated each of the two capitals of the pillars
which stood in front of the portico of the Temple with 200 carvings of the fruit.
Solomon's hope of immortality was proclaimed to all who entered the temple. At a
later date, the silver shekel of Jerusalem in circulation between 143 and 135 BC
had been decorated with an image of a pomegranate.*

*My mind wandered away to the Christian mosaics we had seen earlier that
week, to the pomegranate we thought we had seen in the formal mosaic of a bowl
containing an oil lamp and fruit. It had imprinted itself on my mind simply
because of the red striped vase in which it was contained. Bowl and fruit had stood
within the encircling whorled branches of the mosaic vine tree whose branches
sprawled all over the dome of the basilica of San Clemente. Early Christianity
had assimilated the ancient hope of immortality into its proclamation of the
resurrection of Jesus through the symbols of the vine and the pomegranate. At the
time that the mosaics had been assembled in San Clemente the pomegranate had
also become a symbol of the Church of God, its many seeds held together in one
round fruit.*[1]

*By the time I had reached this point in my reverie we had made our way back
to the site of the catacombs, but the pomegranate tree was not forgotten.*

I have often thought about that beautiful Roman basilica. From the
time of the Acts of the Apostles there had been plenty of dissension

among Christians who engaged in heated arguments during theological debates, especially over the nature of Christ. They even indulged in verbal and physical fights on occasion. When those mosaics were created in the twelfth or thirteenth centuries, visible, structural disunity in the Church, of the kind so well known to our own generation, already existed. Individuals, families and church communities have always struggled to find their unity in Christ in the spirit of Jesus' great high priestly prayer as recorded in the Gospel of St John (John 17). It is all the more wonderful that the artist who conceived the mosaic should have decorated the apse of the basilica with the whole history of salvation in which men and women, going about their familiar occupations, were held within the encircling branches of the vine. From Christ crucified, the true vine, they received the teeming fullness of pardon and new life. The overall impression that the mosaic makes on me is that of Christ's self-sacrificial love that enables all creation to find its home in God's love. His prayer 'that they may all be one' (John 17.21) is the pattern for all intercession for unity.

The human mind has the capacity to combine fragments of thought and memory into a coherent whole. It is this ability to associate different ideas that led me to explore the relationship between the ancient myths about pomegranates and the symbolic portrayal of the vine in San Clemente. The search for the links between them has led directly to the tree of life in the garden of Eden and the tree of life in the heavenly city described in the book of Revelation. In that visionary document is to be found both the hope of immortality and the hope of eventual visible unity in Christ's body, the Christian community of the Church.

When Adam and Eve were expelled from the garden of Eden the cherubim and a flaming sword barred their way back to the tree of life. Yet in succeeding ages prophets and apocalyptic writers came to believe that Yahweh would one day open the way back to that tree. So, for instance, Ezekiel's vision of the New Jerusalem, the heavenly city, reconstitutes the garden of Eden with its river and two trees. In it he writes eloquently of the river of life which will bring health wherever it goes (Ezekiel 47.9) and then says:

> On the banks, on both sides of the river, there will grow all kinds of trees for food. Their leaves will not wither nor their fruit fail, but they will bear fresh fruit every month, because the water for them flows from the sanctuary. Their fruit will be for food and their leaves for healing. (Ezekiel 47.12)

It was upon this prophetic picture that the author of the book of Revelation built his vision of the new garden of Eden in a new age, and in the New Jerusalem. His river comes, not from the sanctuary of the Temple, which would have been destroyed by the time he wrote, but from the throne of God and of the Lamb (Revelation 22.1). Then he continues:

> On either side of the river is the tree of life with its twelve kinds of fruit, producing its fruit each month; and the leaves of the tree are for the healing of the nations. (Revelation 22:2)[2]

In the next verse the message becomes as clear as crystal. In this new city, God's city, which is still to come, the water of life coming from the throne of God, the water coming from Christ's side, will abolish the curse of destruction, the curse incurred by Adam and Eve in the first garden of Eden:

> Nothing accursed will be found there any more. But the throne of God and of the Lamb will be in it, and his servants will worship him; they will see his face, and his name will be on their foreheads. And there will be no more night; they need no light of lamp or sun, for the Lord God will be their light, and they will reign for ever and ever. (Revelation 22.3–5)

Those who believe that Christ's resurrection, ascension and universal presence has united time and eternity also believe that they are brought into the New Jerusalem through baptism. Even though sin constitutes a barrier to the experience of union with God, Christians hold to the objective belief that from the time they are baptized they *are* dwelling in the heavenly city. They will know the fullness of the beatific vision only when they are made holy enough by God to see him face to face: meantime they can catch a glimpse of his glory. They can also be healed by the river of life, and by the leaves of the tree of life whose leaves are for the healing of the nations (Revelation 22.2).

Apocalyptic visions were common at the time when the book of Revelation was written. The Jewish writer of the second book of Esdras, writing at about the same time, says:

> For unto you Paradise is opened, the tree of life is planted, the future age is prepared, plenty is provided, a city is built, a rest is appointed, good works perfected, and wisdom perfected beforehand. The root of evil is sealed up for you, infirmity is extinct, and death is hidden; Hades and corruption have fled away into oblivion, sorrows have passed away, and finally the treasure of immortality is displayed.[3]

Immortality is not part of the Christian gospel but eternal life is. It is a gift from Christ into whose eternal life we are incorporated through baptism. St Paul uses the image of a body to describe the relationship between the whole and its parts (1 Corinthians 12.12–27). The author of St John's Gospel uses the image of another plant, the vine, to explain the relationship between Christ and his disciples. In John's great discourse of chapter 15 Christ tells his disciples that he is the true vine; his Father is the vinedresser who prunes and cuts away the branches that do not bear fruit. He makes the relationship between the stem and its branches clear:

> 'I am the vine, you are the branches. Those who abide in me and I in them bear much fruit, because apart from me you can do nothing. Whoever does not abide in me is thrown away like a branch and withers; such branches are gathered, thrown into the fire, and burned. If you abide in me, and my words abide in you, ask for whatever you wish, and it will be done for you.' (John 15.5–7)

It is this objective incorporation into Christ, the true vine, that makes it possible for Christians to feel themselves to be part of a whole in communion with each other. They are separate branches of the vine and yet the same sap runs through them, the same root and stem supply them with nourishment, the same earth becomes their common home. The leaves on the branches are separate leaves, with particular individual characteristics and yet they are all identifiable as coming from the same plant. The fruits of the vine are grapes, grapes which can be eaten as they are, dried for future use, or made into wine.

Within these double images of the pomegranate tree and the vine are contained the truths that can make reconciliation between human beings a reality: the truth that we are all citizens of the New Jerusalem, the Church, the Body of Christ, the true vine, and the truth that since we are enclosed in Christ as a branch is incorporated into the trunk of a tree, as a pomegranate seed is enclosed in the leathery skin of the fruit, we are part of a united whole, part of each other.

That is the objective truth, the reality of our citizenship of heaven, and yet it is also true that throughout Christian history up to the present time there have been and are visible divisions among Christians who constitute the Church on earth. They are a scandal. They weaken Christian witness. They lead to war. Nevertheless, there *is* a deeper reality; that reality is proclaimed by all the trinitarian Churches when they accept the validity of each other's baptismal rites.

Once the truth of our oneness in Christ has been seen objectively it is impossible to feel alienated from other Christians, even though they do not appear to share the same beliefs, carry out the same rituals, adhere to the same rules of conduct as we do ourselves. As soon as the truth has been assimilated into experience it feels ridiculous to refrain from praying together, eating together, working together.

Unity in Christ overrides institutional disunity. This sense of unity is a prime factor in many people's attempts to foster reconciliation between themselves and their enemies, or between people who are traditional enemies.

'I am the vine', Christ said, 'You are the branches ... You did not choose me, but I chose you. And I appointed you to go and bear fruit, fruit that will last, so that the Father will give you whatever you ask him in my name. I am giving you these commands so that you may love one another' (John 15.5, 16b–17). As the seeds of the pomegranate fruit are held in the sweet flesh of the fruit, until the fruit splits and they are spilled out on to the ground, so those who abide in Christ's love are sent out into the world by him to sow the seeds of his love wherever they go.

The task of finding each other within the love of Christ, the sweet flesh of the pomegranate tree, the root and stem of the vine, is not confined to denominational and inter-faith unity. It extends to all humankind. It is this desire for harmony, for peace, for integration, for bliss, that keeps men and women searching for unity within themselves and with each other.

At this point in history there are many Christians who live in that unity with each other. It is these 'grass-roots' Christians who are the pioneers of visible unity, unity which does not depend upon uniformity but upon mutual love and respect for those who are companions in the Body of Christ.

Many Christian people intercede for reconciliation between warring peoples. These Christians cross boundaries of all kinds. You will find them everywhere. Often their work is quite hidden. At one time in recent history you could find Protestant women comforting Roman Catholic women whose husbands and sons had been killed by Ulster Loyalists. You could find Catholic women taking that same practical comfort to Protestant homes where the IRA had gunned down a member of the family. Few people knew about such actions but sometimes such work comes to light. A Methodist woman, for instance, called Sadie Patterson, worked in this way in the Falls Road area of Belfast. Later she was beaten up for it. That is how her work became known.[4] The Peace People, men and women together, Protestant and Catholic, witnessed to their desire for peace with justice by standing together at peace rallies, by praying together and by working together for peace. Their witness, which followed the running down of three small children in the street by a speeding car after a clash with security forces, also made the headlines.[5]

The kind of work that these peacemakers do day after day in a climate where sectarian hatred can be easily whipped up by acts of violence and murder is epitomized by the Corrymeela Community. This community was founded by a Presbyterian minister called Ray Davey who, inspired by what he had seen of the Iona Community in Scotland, Agape in Italy and Taizé in France, had a vision of a similar project in Northern Ireland. In 1946 he wrote:

> Christian Community, in spite of its lamentable divisions and failure, is the only hope for the world. Already it has out-lived many cultures and civilizations. It has done this and will do it again because, in the last analysis, it is the only true community. All other communities, be they relatively good or bad, are transient, relative or sectional, appealing to one particular age, to one section or one race. The Christian Community transcends colour and class, its terms of reference and its motive power are from beyond, outside man himself.[6]

The Corrymeela Community was conceived at a meeting in September 1964. It took place at the Presbyterian Centre at Queen's University, Belfast, where Ray Davey was the chaplain. By 1965 a group of people from that meeting found sufficient funds between them to buy a large white building which stands near the edge of a cliff top on the north coast of Northern Ireland. By dint of enthusiastic fundraising and hard work, Ray Davey and his friends had the place ready by October 1965. At its entrance they placed a handmade notice:

> Corrymeela is a community of Christian men and women from all branches of the Church, who, as individuals and together are committed to healing the many breaches — social, religious and political — which exist in Northern Ireland and throughout the world.[7]

Within three years of its foundation sectarian violence broke out in Northern Ireland. Within nine years more than one thousand people had died, many more had been injured and millions of pounds worth of damage had been caused. Those figures have escalated in the years since then, despite many attempts by many political leaders and ordinary people to find a just peace.

Throughout these years Corrymeela has gone on praying and working for peace by inviting Christians, young and old, from both sides of the divide, to come to 'the hill of harmony'. There they can find temporary but welcome relief from sectarian hatred.[8] As they live together for periods of time they learn to respect and enjoy each other. They catch the Corrymeela spirit. Many take it home with them. As people leave for home they see another handwritten notice:

> Reconciliation must continue and each week more and more people realise that Corrymeela begins when you leave.[9]

Corrymeela is a shining example of practical Christianity. Its witness has extended far beyond the shores of Northern Ireland. Its spirit lives in hundreds of thousands of people who are working for justice and peace in our world. Nor is it alone. The Fellowship of Reconciliation, the Columbanus Community, the Glencree Reconciliation Centre in Dublin, the Quakers, and many individuals are always at work fostering good relationships between people who are natural enemies. Theirs is a long haul, but eventually it will bear fruit.

Corrymeela, Columbanus, Glencree in Dublin[10] are all success stories, at least in the strength of their visible witness. Such success is achieved at the price of much personal suffering, much disappointment, much frustration. Good ideas are often rejected. Imaginative projects are spoilt by opponents. People who have hard hearts simply will not listen to any talk of peace, even if it comes with justice. Some men and women will kill rather than sit down with their brothers and sisters who are of different cultures, faiths, races or denominations. Men like Martin Luther King, who preached reconciliation between black and white people, or Mahatma Gandhi, who urged Hindus and Muslims to live in peace with one another, were ruthlessly assassinated in their time, and such killings continue all over the world today.

In May 1996, for instance, seven Trappist monks were murdered. They had been kidnapped from their monastery in Algeria by Algerian terrorists from the Groupe Islamique Armé. The monks were offered to the French government in exchange for imprisoned Islamic terrorists. When the exchange was not forthcoming, the Trappists' throats were cut. Their superior, Fr Christian de Chergé, anticipated his assassination. Over two years before this event he had written a letter to his family, 'to be opened in the event of my death'. In it he proclaimed his solidarity with his assassin:

> I should like, when the time comes, to have a clear space,
> which would allow me to beg for forgiveness of God
> and of all my fellow human beings,
> and at the same time forgive with all my
> heart the one who would strike me down ...
> This is what I shall be able to do, if God wills —
> Immerse my gaze in that of the Father,
> to contemplate with him his children of Islam just as he sees
> them,
> all shining with the glory of Christ,
> the fruit of his Passion, filled with the
> Gift of the Spirit, whose secret joy will always be to
> establish communion, and to refashion the likeness,
> delighting in the differences.[11]

After thanking God for his life, his family, his friends, his brother Trappists, he concludes:

> And you also, the friend of my final
> moment, who would not be aware of what you were doing.
> Yes, for you also I wish this *thank you* —
> and this *adieu* — to commend you to the God
> whose face I see in yours.
> And may we find each other, happy 'good thieves', in
> Paradise,
> if it please God, the Father of us both. Amen.[12]

Such a testimony lives on in the minds of those who read it. One marvels at the movement of the Holy Spirit who inspired these words and gave Fr de Chergé the love with which to see God's face in that of his enemy.

The work of praying for reconciliation between human beings is not confined to intercession for peace between those who go to war with each other. It is also an essential part of praying and working for Christian unity within the Body of Christ, the Church of God.

Prayer for Christian unity in the Church is also costly. It highlights the need for perseverance in the face of some of the massive obstacles to peace that people in all sorts of conflicts construct between each other. There will always be many failures before even a small success is won.[13] Many projects will come to an untimely death. Such failures and sorrows are part of the work that God asks of those who are called to be 'ambassadors of Christ' (2 Corinthians 5.20). Take, for instance, what

happened to Little Sister Magdeleine of Jesus. She founded her religious
congregation in 1939, so her friend Jean Vanier tells us in his preface to
her biography, 'to bring the good news of love to people in those places
of pain, rejection, isolation and misery where God (and the Church)
appears to be conspicuously absent'.[14] She had founded it in tandem
with Père Voillaume who led a similar community of men.[15] Both
were inspired by the example and work of Charles de Foucauld,
explorer, hermit, missionary, who had been killed in 1916.[16] The
community grew rapidly. Many women who were not Roman
Catholics wanted to become Little Sisters of Jesus, to find their unity
and solidarity with each other through their common love of, and work
for, Jesus in the poor. Little Sister Magdeleine and her non-Roman
Catholic sisters tried their ideas out in practical ways but they ran into
trouble. As her biographer Kathryn Spink says:

> Difficulties arose not least because non-Catholics could not make their
> vows to the Catholic Church. For Little Sister Magdeleine such
> difficulties were not insurmountable. Nor was the solution conversion.
> For her the union of diversity was too valuable. 'Whatever happens, they
> mustn't become Catholic', she would say of those non-Catholics who
> sought to live the vocation of a Little Sister.[17]

The foundress spoke in the spirit of the Taizé Community, which
she had visited in 1948.[18] At Taizé, under the inspired leadership of
Roger Schutz, the brothers were committed to a search for peace and
reconciliation between divided peoples. Believing that example speaks
more loudly than words, they tried to make their community 'a parable
of communion'.[19] At Taizé Roman Catholics were admitted as full
members of the Community even though they could not share the
same Eucharist. Taizé, however, had been founded by a Protestant
pastor: Little Sister Magdeleine was a Roman Catholic who needed the
approval of the Vatican if her congregation was to become officially
established. Her ideas were rejected by the canonical lawyers. She and
her non-Catholic sisters suffered greatly, but they bowed to the
decision. Today the congregation remains Roman Catholic, but their
hospitality to non-Catholics is a shining example of how mutual love
across the boundaries that divide people from each other can transcend
all visible barriers to Christian unity.

Progress towards reconciliation between denominational churches is
slow, yet it continues, often through tiny signs. Some years ago, for
instance, the Anglican Church threw its doors open to members of
trinitarian churches who belong to denominations other than the

Anglican Communion.[20] It invited them to partake of Holy Communion when they came to Anglican churches. Many Christians, Roman Catholics included, have decided that they want to do this as a way of building Christian unity. Others believe that they should not communicate, either because they do not believe in the validity of non-Roman Catholic sacraments, or because they believe that inter-communion can only happen when full communion between the denominations is achieved. So they abstain with regret but will often come to the altar rails to kneel in solidarity with their Anglican neighbours.

Over fifty years ago Roman Catholics were forbidden to pray with other Christians, even at civic services.[21] Since then the ecumenical scene has greatly changed. Members of all denominations are encouraged to pray with each other, except in areas where sectarian hatred prevails. Notably, even in those localities, there are some places where Christians break down the barriers and worship together.

In 1972 the Roman Catholic Church decided that in certain particular instances their priests and eucharistic ministers could administer the sacraments to Christians who were not Roman Catholics. Provided that the non-Catholics greatly desired to receive the sacraments, freely requested them, manifested a faith which the Roman Catholic Church professes with regard to these sacraments and were unable to have recourse to a minister of their own community they were allowed to share in Holy Communion at a Roman Catholic Mass. In the encyclical *Ut Unum Sint*, published in 1995, Pope John Paul II left out the fourth condition. This encyclical opens the way to real opportunities for building bridges across denominational divides.[22] It places an official blessing on practices that have been commonplace in some places for many years. These have brought healing to many non-Roman Catholics who share the Catholic doctrine of the Eucharist, but who do not feel called to join the Roman Catholic Church in order to participate in its sacraments on occasion. They rejoice in its welcome when they are away from their own local Christian worship community.

Individuals and groups of people who have found their unity with each other in Christ become signs of love and unity in a world which is more accustomed to disunity and hatred. They are examples to the rest of us who are still struggling to find that unity. St Paul, always a practical man, tells us how to go about finding our home in Love, and with each other. After telling members of the Church in Colossae that through baptism they have put on a new self which 'is being renewed in knowledge according to the image of its Creator' (Colossians 3.10) he points out that in that image there is no distinction between people of different races, religions, cultures and social classes, for, he says, 'Christ is all and in all' (Colossians 3.11b). Then he goes on to give the disciples some practical advice:

> As God's chosen ones, holy and beloved, clothe yourselves with compassion, kindness, humility, meekness and patience. Bear with one another and, if anyone has a complaint against another, forgive each other; just as the Lord has forgiven you, so you must also forgive. Above all clothe yourselves with love, which binds everything together in perfect harmony. And let the peace of Christ rule in your hearts to which indeed you were called in the one body. And be thankful. (Colossians 3.12–15).

That all sounds very easy, but as every disciple of Christ knows it is not. We have to wait for a long time, sometimes many years, before we are given insight into the mystery of our reconciliation with God through Christ's work on the cross. Once we have experienced that truth we will naturally want to be reconciled to our fellow human beings. We may have to wait still longer before God gives us the gift of interior peace which can carry us into the work of helping other people to find their unity with each other. Yet if we are faithful, keep searching, and are willing to be pruned of all that hinders us from finding that unity with each other in God, we shall become the kind of people that God wants us to be.

The search for interior peace and unity in individuals has been placed at the end of this exploration rather than at the beginning. That is not to despise the needs of individuals but to say that they cannot be fulfilled at the expense of their membership of a corporate body. Navel gazing and detachment from 'the affairs of men' is not part of God's ultimate purposes for those who are created in the image and likeness of God. The most ardent, enclosed and geographically isolated anchorite, contemplative nun or imprisoned saint is never separated from his or her fellow human beings because they are together in Christ. Nevertheless, we are individuals and we do matter to God as such. If we begin with a strong and firm understanding of our unity with all people in Christ we shall be able to find unity inside ourselves the more easily.

The task of integrating the disparate elements in our own personalities may seem to be an impossible one. It is — if we think of it as a matter of self-improvement and try to accomplish it in our own strength — but with God's help all things are possible. Such a task involves self-forgetfulness, self-sacrifice and a thirst for God that enables us to put Father, Son and Holy Spirit at the centre of our lives so that we are continually living within God's commandments and seeking to see all creation within God's love.

To undertake this journey towards union with God is not an easy task. For, after all, sin lurks in all of us and its pleasures are always there, ready to divert us from the purity of heart and single-mindedness that are necessary precursors to union with God. The journey from egotism to God-centredness will bring us into conflict with sin in an infinite number of its disguises. The approach to God's peace is littered with mirages that our pride has invented to tempt us to believe that we have arrived at our goal when in reality we are a thousand miles from it. As we get nearer to God we may attract the hatred of those who hate and despise the image of God in themselves and so seek to make us sin. They will tempt us to judge them. If we do, we know that we are still a million miles from our destiny.

Isaac of Nineveh, the seventh-century Syrian whose influence is particularly noticeable in Russian spirituality, has given all disciples of Christ a simple way of measuring themselves against his example. He said:

> Let yourself be persecuted but do not persecute others.
> Let yourself be crucified but do not crucify others.
> Let yourself be insulted but do not insult others.
> Let yourself be slandered but do not slander others.
> Rejoice with those who rejoice and weep with those who weep.
> Such is the sign of purity.
> Suffer with the sick. Be afflicted with sinners.
> Exalt with those who repent. Be a friend of all.
> But in your spirit remain alone ...
> Spread your cloak over anyone who falls into sin and shield him.
> And if you cannot take his fault on yourself and accept punishment
> in his place, do not destroy his character.[23]

The same teacher was once asked: 'When is a person sure of having arrived at purity?' He answered:

> When he considers all human beings are good, and no created thing appears impure or defiled to him. Then he is truly pure in heart.[24]

By those standards most of us would fail miserably but since we know
that 'God himself is the life of all who participate in him',[25] and since
we believe that our baptism gives us the Holy Spirit by whose grace we
can 'be shaped as a complete copy of the divine nature',[26] we believe by
faith that we *shall* be conformed to the likeness of our Saviour at some
time, whether in this world or the next.

   This is our task — to allow ourselves to become so immersed in God
that we begin to absorb the energy of Love and to radiate it in our lives.
Our search for union with God cannot be undertaken for ourselves
alone. When we arrive at union with God we shall find, as Maximus
the Confessor said in the seventh century, that:

> The spirit that is united to God by prayer and by love acquires wisdom,
> goodness, power, beneficence, generosity . . . in a word, that person bears
> the attributes of God.[27]

   The search for interior unity demands rigorous honesty. If we cannot
forgive others, we cannot be forgiven. If we cannot forgive ourselves,
we cannot feel God's forgiveness. If we cannot receive God's
forgiveness, we cannot receive it from other people. If we hate others,
we will invite their hatred. If we hate ourselves, we will be unable to
love ourselves for God's sake. If we think God hates us we will not be
able to receive his love. If we live in disharmony, in conflict, we shall
find ourselves in fragments. If we keep our thoughts and feelings in
compartments we shall be unable to act in good faith as a whole and
integrated human being. God wants us all to dwell enclosed in Love. If
we are patient God will accomplish in us that which he desires. We will
become co-workers with Jesus in the task of bringing in the kingdom.
We will become God's ambassadors. We will become people who are at
peace with themselves and who see others in the light of the peace of
God that passes all understanding. We will become people who radiate
peace, who create an atmosphere in which other people can find their
peace. We are called to bring Christ into the midst of warring people.
His presence draws people to himself. It is he who enables them to find
peace with justice between themselves. This is a great mystery but it
does happen, and whenever it does we will realize that we have been
privileged to see Christ at work. We fall down and worship God. Then
we must get up and resume our own journey.

Part Three

The fruits of intercession

Malus domestica. Symbol of Christ — the apple tree.

7

The fruitful tree

THE RESULTS OF INTERCESSION

'My Father is glorified by this, that you bear much fruit and become my disciples.' (John 15.8)

The fruit of the spirit is love, joy, peace, patience, kindness, generosity, faithfulness, gentleness and self-control. There is no law against such things. And those who belong to Christ Jesus have crucified the flesh with its passions and desires. If we live by the Spirit, let us also be guided by the Spirit. Let us not become conceited, competing against one another, envying one another. (Galatians 5.22–26)

'It has been a good summer', my friend said as we strolled through the convent garden.

'The fruit trees are laden', I remarked.

'The nuns will have enough apples and plums this year to feed them through the winter.'

I smiled inwardly. I remembered my years with the nuns at the convent. Harvest time had always been a time of intense effort.

Each year it all started when the sister in charge of the fruit began to clean out the cool underground cellar where they would stack the apples and pears on the neat wooden slats that ran all round the wall. There was much scrubbing of the shelving and the floors. Soon afterwards every sister who could work would be dispatched to gather in the fruit. It was a time of toil, weary arms and backs, and general tiredness.

By the end of harvest time the cellar shelves were full with the best apples and pears. The less perfect apples were turned into frozen purée. Plums were bottled, frozen, or made into jam. For a few weeks there was a glut of fruit in the refectory. Some years there was so much of it that the sisters had difficulty inventing new ways to serve it up to their guests.

When I had been a nun I sometimes found myself so satiated with fruit that I positively disliked the sight of the piled-high bowl in the refectory. Now that I was away from the convent and living alone in a town house without a proper garden I generally ate only the cheapest fruit I could buy. Sometimes friends would bring offerings from their gardens; I ate everything with thankful reverence.

My reminiscences were interrupted by my companion's voice.

'It's easy to see rich harvest here', she said. 'I see the results of all the hard labour that the sisters put into their garden work; but what about the fruit of their prayer? The sisters spend hours and hours on their knees in prayer for the world, and what good does it do? The world doesn't seem to change all that much as a result. What's the point of all this intercessory prayer?' Her voice sounded rather fierce, almost accusatory.

'I don't know what good it does. I think they would say, and I certainly do say, that we pray because we are prompted to pray by the Holy Spirit. We can't help it. We don't look for results. It's just something that Christians feel impelled to do.'

We heard the bell summoning us to chapel for the next service. We walked across the grass: questions still hung in the air, but they would have to wait.

Some people never question intercession: they are convinced of its efficacy. Some people begin to intercede because they are encouraged by those who testify that their prayers to God have been answered, that they have been given what they wanted. God is often very kind to us, knowing, perhaps that many human beings do need good results to bolster their faith. Positive and tangible results do often follow prayer. People are converted. They are healed. Wars do cease. Injustices are remedied. Others, however, are more sceptical. They know that their prayers are not always answered as they had hoped. To them it is natural to question even such a central activity as intercession. What, then, are the fruits of such prayer?

In the Bible intercession is never a neutral activity. People who came to Jesus and pleaded with him for healing, either for themselves or for others, did not say 'I don't mind if you heal me or not'. They knew what they wanted. Jairus, for instance, came to Jesus, fell at his feet and 'begged him to come to his house, for he had an only daughter, about twelve years old, who was dying' (Luke 8.41–42). In another incident in the same Gospel a blind man outside Jericho shouted 'Jesus, son of David, have mercy on me', and went on shouting even though the people nearby tried to silence him:

> Jesus stood still and ordered the man to be brought to him; and when he came near, he asked him, 'What do you want me to do for you?' He said, 'Lord, let me see again.' Jesus said to him, 'Receive your sight; your faith has saved you.' Immediately he regained his sight and followed him, glorifying God; and all the people, when they saw it, praised God. (Luke 18.40–43)

People even argued with Jesus because they felt so strongly about the people for whom they were pleading. The Caananite woman who met an apparently indifferent Jesus overcame his reluctance with her humility and faith when she asked for 'the crumbs that fall from the master's table'. Her daughter was healed (Matthew 15.21–28).

So it is with us too. We are to ask for what we, or those for whom we pray, need. Our requests are specific. We are to persist in our prayer with humility and faith. Sometimes we have to recognize that what people ask us to pray for is not what Christ wants to give them. When, for instance, Peter and John were on their way to the temple a lame man who had been a cripple from birth asked them for money (Acts 3.1–16). Peter recognized his deeper need and healed him from his disability. Then he preached a sermon to all who were astonished at the sight and told them it was the name of Jesus that had 'made this man strong ... and the faith that is through Jesus has given him this perfect health in the presence of all of you' (Acts 3.16).

Fruitful results come to those who pray in the way that Jesus and his early disciples did. Sometimes the fruit will be obvious. It is not wrong for Christians to rejoice when their prayers do seem to bear fruit, good fruit. Few of them fall into the error of attributing the positive results of intercession to their own involvement. They know that such things happen because their prayers have tuned into the mind of Christ. Jesus' power to save those who come to God through him is absolute, 'since he always lives to make intercession for them' (Hebrews 7.25). Christ is always faithful. His disciples' task is to take their petitions, their deepest desires, even at times their apparently trivial requests, to him. Then they leave them with him in total confidence that their prayers will be heard, passed on and responded to in ways that are loving and the best for those for whom the prayer is offered. Whenever we are healed from sin or from physical illness, whenever someone else is healed, whenever injustice is put to flight, whenever people in the world come to their senses and reduce their stockpiles of weapons that are capable of destroying the planet earth, it is right to rejoice. Returning thanks to God in such circumstances is a crucial part of intercessory prayer.

It becomes much harder to go on interceding when there is no obvious fruit coming from such prayer. After all very few people in the world undertake any meaningful endeavour without expecting some positive results. Someone who goes through long training as a medical student hopes to become a doctor. Runners who undergo strenuous training hope to win races. Some achieve their goals, but even those who do not gain their objective will have learnt much from their efforts. However, it is not at all easy to persevere with intercession in the face of doubt, apparent failure, contradiction and scepticism. Many human beings can accept the theory that repeated refusal to fulfil their desires may be a sign of a positive response from an all-sovereign, loving God. In practice, however, some begin to doubt themselves, or even the very existence of God. If they and we are to find a way of dealing with natural disappointment, we will need to look at Christ's teaching and example.

During his earthly ministry Christ taught his disciples to pray to their tender loving Father in heaven. He taught them to pray from within the secret room in the depths of their being, 'Your kingdom come; your will be done on earth as it is in heaven' (Matthew 6.10). All prayer has to be in tune with God's will. That is the starting-point for all earthly intercession. It is the prayer that Jesus prayed in the garden of Gethsemene: 'My Father', he said, 'if it is possible, let this cup pass from me; yet not what I want but what you want' (Matthew 26.39). He prayed this prayer three times before he was at peace, knowing that his prayer would not be answered in the way his humanity wanted. When he returned to his sleeping disciples he displayed a new confidence in the fact that he must suffer death (Matthew 26.45–46).

That kind of confidence can come also to his disciples who are disappointed in their hopes. St Paul pleaded three times that the 'thorn in his flesh' might be removed from him (2 Corinthians 12.7) but it was not to be. The Lord's answer was 'My grace is sufficient for you, for power is made perfect in weakness' (2 Corinthians 12.9).

This attitude of trustful compliance with God's will has been repeated again and again during the last two thousand years. The literature about Christ's healing work in the world is full of success stories. Anyone, however, who reads widely will also find moving accounts of people who have not been cured in the way they hoped they would be, but who, nevertheless, have been healed. Joni Eareckson, for instance, was seventeen years old in 1967 when she dived into shallow water and broke her neck. Her spinal cord was severed. She was left paralysed in all four limbs. She and her Christian friends prayed with great earnestness. They asked for her complete healing. They believed that this could happen, even that it was God's will that it should happen. They even bargained with God. They told God that it would be enough if she regained the use of her hands. Joni describes how she felt when God did not respond as she had hoped:

When I didn't regain my hands, I felt betrayed. God had let me down. So
I was angry at God. In order to get back at Him, I discovered a way to
shut Him out along with the rest of the world. I went into moody,
depressive, fantasy 'trips.' I'd sleep late in order to daydream and
fantasize. By concentrating hard, I was able to completely shut out the
present and reality.[1]

This rebellion continued for a considerable length of time before Joni
saw that she was not getting anywhere by persisting with these negative
thoughts. Two years after her accident, still completely paralysed from
the neck downwards, she met a young preacher, Steve Estes. He helped
her to find new attitudes towards her predicament. It took time, but
eventually Joni was able to see that in heaven she would be released
from her paralysis, given a new body and freed. Once she had seen this
truth she was able to see her wheelchair 'more as a tool than a tragedy'.[2]
Accepting her weakness and powerlessness, Joni relied wholly on God's
grace. She went on to develop a wonderful ministry of preaching and
writing and helped many people to find faith. She painted pictures with
her mouth, wrote several very influential books and she was blessed
with a happy marriage. In her first book, written seven years after her
accident, she says:

> I saw that my injury was not a tragedy but a gift God was using to help
> me to conform to the image of Christ, something that would mean my
> ultimate satisfaction, happiness — even joy.[3]

Such faith is precious. It is also inspiring. Yet many of us still find it
extremely difficult to come to terms with misfortune and apparently
unanswered prayers. This is largely because we do not know whether to
go on praying for what we believe is good, or whether to stop and begin
believing that what we are asking for is not according to God's present
will.

In the case of severe illness God's will usually becomes apparent in a
relatively short space of time. A woman hears, for instance, that a friend
has cancer. She prays for him to be cured. He has a major operation and
appears to be making a good recovery. She rejoices. She gives thanks
and surrounds him with regular prayer. Eighteen months later she hears
that her friend has extensive secondaries. She continues to pray for his
healing. It becomes evident that he is not going to recover and so she
changes her prayer and begins to pray for him to die so that his
sufferings can be at an end. He dies. God's will for him has been made
evident over a period of two years. Such a sequence of events is not
unusual. However, it is not always like that.

Sometimes people have to pray 'Thy kingdom come, thy will be done' for many years without knowing what the outcome of their prayers will be. Sometimes the whole endeavour seems to be so prolonged that they have to heed Jesus' words in Mark's Gospel and add fasting to their prayer. By doing this they believe that they help God to drive away the evil that presents an obstacle to the coming of the kingdom (Mark 9.29).

Fasting does not necessarily mean fasting from food. It may mean fasting from one's pride and sense of propriety by an act of solidarity or witness with the people for whom one is praying. It may mean abstaining from using the same weapons against the oppressors that they use in order to keep their victims submissive. Leaders like Mahatma Gandhi, Helder Câmara and Martin Luther King, for instance, always urged that all witness and protest should be made without violence. It seemed to them wrong to use evil means to bring about a right end. Gandhi and King were immensely influential in their respective struggles for the freedom of their people. Both were assassinated by those who despised their stance. Helder Câmara lived on but attempts were made by his own Church to silence him. Today, much of his work appears to have been swept away, yet he and others continue to pray for the liberation of their people. Reformers who do not believe in fasting from violence may have to suffer greatly for their beliefs before they achieve good objectives.

The true cost of intercession, public protest and witness is measured in untold, often hidden, suffering, even loss of life. This is well illustrated in the struggle against slavery and racism.

For many generations a substantial number of sincere and devout Christians accepted the existence of slavery. Many of them actually owned slaves. Some of them used the accounts of slavery in the Bible to justify their behaviour. Some slave owners treated their slaves very well, but many transported their human cargo in highly inhuman conditions. Many slaves died. Many more died at the hands of cruel and exploitative slave owners. Led by people like John Newton, Thomas Clarkson and William Wilberforce, thousands of people prayed, worked and suffered to abolish slavery. It was not until the nineteenth century that it was outlawed in England and in the United States of America.

The abolition of slavery did not bring about its ending. It still exists in parts of the world. The struggle also left another legacy, that of racism. Christians were among those who continued to hold to the dogma that white-skinned human beings were superior in intelligence and qualities of character to black-skinned people. In some parts of the world anyone with a black or brown skin was automatically deprived of any right to vote in elections. They were denied good education, exploited at work, moved forcibly from desirable housing areas and resettled in townships that were bleak and far away from the city centres where most black-skinned men had to work. In other parts of the world the conditions under which black and coloured men and women had to live and work were appalling.

The struggle against structural apartheid in South Africa and the southern states of the United States of America took so long that many Christians praying for its end in the early and middle part of the twentieth century died before they saw any positive result from their prayer. They, like others who survived to see the end of legislative discrimination against black and coloured people, would have heard arguments from devout Christians to say that if their prayers and work were not answered it meant that God permitted the enshrinement by law of differences among races.

The work of changing oppressive attitudes and social customs continues. Christians who are alive today who began to pray for change to come some fifty years ago needed the grace of clear sight and great perseverance if they were to believe that they were right in regard to their desire for change. At that time, just after the ending of the Second World War, many leading Christians in all churches were remarkably apathetic towards racism. Many unconsciously upheld it by electing white-skinned people to their legislative assemblies without a thought that there might be suitable people with a different skin colour. Others were openly racist. The fact that they sometimes acted with benign paternalism towards those whom they oppressed did not make it any less unpleasant for those whom they subjugated.

It was in this kind of climate that some Christians who believed that all racism was wrong, and that apartheid was the epitome of error, joined together to pray and work for its ending. Their prayer, work and witness had to continue for generation after generation.[4] For many years it was disheartening to see so little change in society. Many people died before their prayers were answered. Some must have felt that God was deaf, others that God was powerless against the forces of evil. Others, thinking that they were in the wrong, simply gave up. In the end, and after much collective suffering, even unto death, they were vindicated. Structural apartheid in the United States of America came to an end gradually. That in South Africa virtually came to an end with the release of Nelson Mandela from imprisonment in 1992.[5]

The day that Nelson Mandela was freed in South Africa after more than a quarter of a century's imprisonment marked the time when justice overcame prejudice. On that day an enclosed nun, who some thirty years before had lived and worked in South Africa alongside Trevor Huddleston as he stood in solidarity with black and Coloured people of that country, sat by the flickering screen of an ancient television set in a remote convent deep in the heart of Britain. The tears of joy that trickled down her cheeks spoke of the relief that she and many other people must have felt when they heard the news. Their prayers had been answered at long last.

Nelson Mandela became president of his country. His generosity towards people who had formerly been his enemies was inspiring. Yet racism is by no means conquered anywhere in the world. Prayer and action have to continue until it does end.

Prolonged intercession of this kind can bring its own special fruit. Doubt as to whether or not one is praying in tune with God's will can in fact strengthen faith. Delay in achieving the fulfilment of desirable hopes can lead to a deeper appreciation of the complexity of the situation and a deeper compassion for the opponents of change. A person who pleads with God on behalf of others over a long period of time may and often does bear fruit, the fruit of the spirit, 'love, joy, peace, patience, kindness, generosity, faithfulness, gentleness and self-control' (Galatians 5.22). That in itself is a victory over evil. It is more than that, for a person who bears fruit makes it available to others. When others taste that fruit they often want to become the kind of people who can bear the same fruit and share it with other people.

A loving person can inspire others to be loving, even though he or she may also attract hatred as well. Someone who communicates a sense of joy even in the midst of great suffering reminds us of Christ, 'who for the sake of the joy that was set before him endured the cross, disregarding its shame' (Hebrews 12.2). 'Make peace within you', said St Seraphim, 'and a thousand will find their peace around you.'[6] It is a great gift to impart a sense of peace to other people. And so it is with kindness, goodness and all the other fruit of the Spirit.

Although one fruit of intercession is undoubtedly the increase of goodness in the world it is also sadly true that virtue is repellent to the forces of evil in the world. Intercessors must expect some attack, either from those who scoff, undermine and taunt, or from the 'cosmic powers of this present darkness ... the spiritual forces of evil in the heavenly places' (Ephesians 6.12).

Spiritual warfare may be an unexpected but real fruit of intercessory prayer. Some intercessors seem to be more engaged with the devil than others, but all are liable to attack, often in very subtle ways. The only way to deal with evil, from whatever source it comes, is to ignore the evil and focus on the person of Jesus. No evil can withstand direct encounter with Christ. The more an intercessor becomes a channel for God's grace, a channel of God's love, a way by which Christ enters the world, the more evil is put to flight. It may not look that way initially, as we can see from the story of Archbishop Oscar Romero.

In 1977 an oppressive regime in El Salvador, Central America, began to deal ruthlessly with those who protested at the social injustices that were being inflicted on the ordinary poor people of that country by a powerful and rich élite. Over a period of several years Christian priests, nuns and lay people had begun to support the poorest and most oppressed people of their country, the *campesinos*, the peasants, who were trying to band together in unions to improve their standard of living. As protest and dissent grew the government stepped up its policy of eliminating all who opposed them. Priests were murdered. Handbills were circulated by right-wing government supporters saying 'Be a patriot, kill a priest'.[7] More priests and young Christian leaders were tortured and killed.

Throughout this time Oscar Romero, by now Archbishop of San Salvador, preached peace. On one occasion in 1977 when a church in Aguilares had been ransacked, the tabernacle desecrated, four foreign Jesuit priests tortured and expelled from the country, many other people killed and injured, Romero asked those who had been spared 'to pray to the Lord for forgiveness and for due repentance of those who turned this town into a prison and a place of torture'.[8] He continued to urge his people to 'oppose brute force and psychological warfare with truth and love'.[9]

In the three years of life left to him the Archbishop of San Salvador became a champion of the poor, a formidable critic of unjust feudal laws and a preacher of the gospel to everyone who would hear. Many of his own colleagues, including some fellow bishops and the papal nuncio, found him a great irritant and a nuisance. They tried to have him removed.[10] Archbishop Romero's popularity among the people was so great that these attempts failed, but his enemies steadily increased. They felt he had to be silenced. He continued to speak out for the poor. He knew very well that he risked assassination by doing so. He went on, always preaching forgiveness and reconciliation, always praying for those who opposed him and who continued to oppress the poor and to kill their supporters.

At last, on 25 March 1980, just after he finished preaching at a requiem Mass for the mother of one of his friends, he was killed by a single bullet. No one was ever charged with his murder, which was widely believed to have been organized by the government of the day.

Before he died Oscar Romero had written:

> You may say, if they succeed in killing me, that I pardon and bless those who do the deed. Would that they might be convinced that they are wasting their time! A bishop will die, but the Church of God, which is the people, will never perish.[11]

His words came true. The poor thought him to be a saint and prayed to him. Even though it is true that the killings went on, that in the first two years after his death 35,000 Salvadoreans perished in the civil war, that his death seemed to have achieved nothing, he has become a symbol to all who struggle for social justice throughout the world. The poor canonized him immediately. In March 1990 the Roman Catholic Church began the formal process for his official beatification.

Evil can kill the body. It cannot destroy the soul. It cannot obliterate good. It cannot stop God. Those who pray must be prepared to bear fruit through righteous action, and when they do they will help Christ to bring in the kingdom of God. This truth applies as much to Christians praying quietly in their homes for their neighbours as it does to the El Salvadoreans protesting on the streets. If one listens to what God is saying, if one pleads with God for other people, sooner or later one will find oneself speaking out on their behalf. It may bring one suffering, it may bring apparent failure, but, providing that one has the mind of Christ (1 Corinthians 2.16), it will in the end help Christ to bring in the kingdom of God.

What does all this mean in practical terms to a man or woman praying at home in a safe environment, at a far distance from physical danger yet united in prayer with those who suffer from evil? It means that we in our homes will experience some of the pressures and pains that are taking place in another part of the world. It means that we will be assaulted from time to time by a sense of being oppressed by dark heaviness, the heaviness of sin and cosmic evil. Our 'speaking out' will be to refuse to collude with that evil, to refuse to sin in our own environment, to resist the small temptations that come to us in our daily lives with all the strength at our command, that is the strength given to us by the Holy Spirit.

Imagine, for instance that you are a nun in a convent. You are living in close contact with other people, some of whom you do not find naturally congenial. One of them who is senior to you criticizes you again and again. You cannot get away from her. The feelings of inadequacy you have in this situation begin to resonate with the feelings that another person is experiencing in prison in a far distant country. You are drawn together in God's eternal time — so different from spatial time and place — through your intercession for those who are under interrogation in prison. If you resist the temptation to believe that you are as hopelessly inadequate as the senior nun appears to you to be trying to make you feel, if you keep your dignity and integrity and refuse to revile her in return, then you are 'speaking out' for all oppressed peoples. You are refusing to allow evil to invade you and make you behave as your oppressor is doing. You are winning a victory for God, not only in your own convent situation, but also in a far away country, where your own resistance can help to reinforce another person's morale. This is the mystery of mutuality within the Body of Christ and it is nowhere more keenly felt than in the work of intercession, be it in a convent or in a family home in a peaceful country or in a tormented place of terror in a war-torn part of God's world.

Those who can understand this mystery of mutuality within the Body of Christ are those who know the truth of St Paul's great passage on the inter-relationship of parts of the body with the whole (1 Corinthians 12.12 – 13.13). In it are to be found these words: 'If one member suffers, all suffer together with it; if one member is honoured, all rejoice together with it' (12.26).

Understanding that mystery is a fruit of intercession. Putting it into practice is a way of claiming victory for Christ and a source of great thankfulness to God.

Phoenix dactylifera. The date palm, sign of victory and source of thanksgiving.

8

The palm tree

The next day the great crowd of people that had come to the festival heard that Jesus was coming to Jerusalem. So they took branches of palm trees and went out to meet him, shouting:

> 'Hosanna!
> Blessed is the one who comes in
>   the name of the Lord —
>   the King of Israel.' (John 12.12–13)

After this I looked, and there was a great multitude that no one could count, from every nation, from all tribes and peoples and languages, standing before the throne and before the Lamb, robed in white, with palm branches in their hands. (Revelation 7.9)

Nine months after the death of my husband I went on pilgrimage to the Holy Land to ask God to show me how I should spend my own remaining years.

I went with a close friend. Neither of us knew any of the other people in our party. One day the group celebrated the Eucharist together by the shore of the Lake of Galilee. As we walked slowly down to the cleared space in the heart of a small thicket of trees, I noticed an abundance of palm trees; a verse of a familiar psalm flickered through my mind:

> The righteous flourish like the palm tree,
>   and grow like a cedar in Lebanon,
> They are planted in the house of the Lord;
>   they flourish in the courts of our God.
> In old age they still produce fruit;
>   they are always green and full of sap,
> showing that the Lord is upright;
>   he is my rock, and there is no unrighteousness in him.
> (Psalm 92.12–15)

At the time I neither felt that I was flourishing, nor could I contemplate aloneness as a way of bearing fruit in old age. As for Yahweh being a rock ... at that moment I felt as if I were standing on shifting sand.

The Eucharist began. I scarcely heard the familiar words of the priest. My mind had focused on the trees. The evergreen cedars were a symbol of grandeur, durability, majesty, eternal life. Palm trees were a sign of victory:

'Death has been swallowed up in victory.'
'Where, O death, is your victory?
Where, O death, is your sting?' (1 Corinthians 15.54–55)

Suddenly in my mind I was no longer in Galilee but sitting with a group of African Christians under a date palm in Liberia. With the exception of myself, all of them were lepers. I had come to dispense medicine, to give the older ones painful injections of the chaulmoogra oil they were used to: the younger ones were given the more expensive, newly developed wonder pills. When the medical work was finished we would settle down to worship. I would preach, teach catechism, and settle problems. At nightfall we would all drink palm wine and enjoy a thanksgiving feast together. That night, I remembered with a shudder, the feast had consisted of freshly killed chicken fried in palm oil and the local delicacy of de-winged flying termites. Missionaries of my day closed their eyes and swallowed whatever they were given: it would have been the height of rudeness to refuse. During the meal the conversation turned to the subject of death . . . Jesus' entry into Jerusalem and his death on a cross, and death in a village in Africa, a familiar event.

'It's a victory', I had said with all the confident ignorance of my youth. At that moment I heard the high-pitched moaning wails of the women. I knew it meant that Moses, one of the lepers, had just died. He would be buried almost immediately. I would be there.

'Will he have arms in heaven?' I was asked.

'If he needs them. We don't know what our resurrection bodies will be like, you know', I explained. 'He'll be free, free in a way he hasn't been for these thirty years.' By the end of his life all that had remained of this leper's arms were two withered stumps above where his elbows had been. He had no feet, no nose and a terribly scarred face. He was blind.

'We must welcome sister death', I said. 'For Moses, victory has come at last. Thank God that he is with Christ, free from his old body, free at last.'

How easy I had found it to say those words. Death was so common in that small outpost in Africa that grief was acute and noisy for a few hours, but it was short-lived. Moses would not disappear from his widow's consciousness but she would quickly resume her duties in the community.

'Now', I thought, 'now it's me and how different I feel about it all.'

My mind came back to present reality, to the palms by the shores of the lake. The priest had reached the Gospel. I forced myself to attend. It was, I noted without surprise, the story of Jesus and the ten lepers, only one of whom, an

outcast Samaritan, finding himself cured, returned to give thanks (Luke 17.11–
19). 'Then Jesus asked, "Were not ten made clean? But the other nine, where
are they? Was none of them found to return and give praise to God except this
foreigner"' (Luke 17.17–18).

The words reproached me. I felt guilty. Then, almost simultaneously, I
realized that I had a lifetime's happiness to give thanks for. Why then should
I not give thanks for this time of cruel loneliness that might yet bring great
blessing? Had I not prayed that God would take my husband out of his
suffering? My prayer had been answered. Now he was in a new mode of
existence. One day I too would be freed in the same way. Should I return to God
and give thanks? I did.

In this true story we see one person being helped to the realization that
thanksgiving is an integral part of intercession. Christians are taught to
give thanks 'at all times and in all places'.[1] If those words are to be taken
literally then they mean what they say: we, like Job, are to bless God,
whatever happens to us. When God permitted Satan to afflict Job and
his whole family and then struck Job with malignant ulcers from the
sole of his feet to the top of his head, Job refused to reproach God. His
wife protested:

'Do you still persist in your integrity? Curse God, and die.' But he said to
her, 'You speak as any foolish woman would speak. Shall we receive the
good at the hand of God, and not receive the bad?' In all this Job did not
sin with his lips. (Job 2.9–10)

St Paul, too, urges us to rejoice in all circumstances. He speaks from
his own experience of many hardships and sorrows borne for the sake
of Christ:

Rejoice in the Lord always; again I will say, Rejoice. Let your gentleness
be known to everyone. The Lord is near. Do not worry about anything,
but in everything by prayer and supplication with thanksgiving let your
requests be made known to God. And the peace of God, which surpasses
all understanding, will guard your hearts and minds in Christ Jesus.
(Philippians 4.4–7)

Sometimes these encouraging statements have led people to assume false
smiles during times of terrible misery, to think that they must never cry
at funerals, to 'grin and bear it' in heroic ways. While some people may
retain a genuine sense of Christ's nearness with them at all times and in
all places, even in terrible circumstances, many of us will not. Our misery
is real. It shows. Our petitions to God are anguished, making us feel close
to Christ's agony in the garden of Gethsemene when his sweat 'fell to the

ground like great drops of blood' (Luke 22.44). Our pain becomes evident in our faces. Yet throughout our suffering we may be aware of a spirit of joy and thankfulness at a deeper level of our being.

This kind of thankfulness comes to us whenever we recognize that our sufferings are taken by Christ, united with his and changed into joy. As the author of Hebrews says:

> Let us run with perseverance the race that is set before us, looking to Jesus the pioneer and perfecter of our faith, who for the sake of the joy that was set before him endured the cross, disregarding the shame, and has taken his seat at the right hand of the throne of God. (Hebrews 12.2)

As we share in his sufferings so we share in the victory, not only after death but here on earth as well.

This kind of joy in suffering for Christ's sake on earth has partly been described in the chapter on double-sided or Janus prayer and in the last chapter (see pp. 26–33 and pp. 103–11). In that kind of prayer there is a simultaneous perception of good and evil, pain and joy. In someone who has learnt to rejoice at all times there comes a deeper knowledge still. Their union with Christ means that they are able to participate in the Eucharist and in eucharistic life with utter simplicity and confidence in his victory over evil and death. What they know by experience, we too may know by faith.

It is this participation in the Eucharist that is central to all intercession. Christ's saving self-sacrifice took place 'once and for all' in time, at a place, Golgotha outside Jerusalem. Yet in eternity, in ways that, being time-bound, we can scarcely imagine, he enacts that sacrifice of thanksgiving and salvation anew. We who are on earth can reach heaven, eternal life, through joining in his perpetual prayer since 'he lives for ever to intercede' for us and for all humankind (Hebrews 7.25). We reach him, either by lifting up our hearts in solitary and group prayer, or by our attendance at a Eucharist on earth.

In private or small group prayer we are always in touch with the Eucharist in heaven through the activity of the Holy Spirit in us who 'intercedes with sighs too deep for words' (Romans 8.26), but some of us find it difficult to realize that in our hearts. However, whenever we join in a celebration of the Eucharist on earth we are visibly assured of being in touch with the Eucharist in heaven. That is an objective reality. We do not need to question ourselves about the quality or efficacy of our prayers because we can see Christ in action through the dramatic re-enactment of his saving work on the cross. We can be in touch with his life-giving presence when we receive him in Holy

Communion. Hence the intercessions at such a Eucharist have special significance.

Intercessory prayer is the task of the whole gathered community at the Eucharist, priest and people together. It is fitting that our petitions be offered by a lay person, or group of lay people, since this is one of the main ways in which they affirm the priesthood of the laity in public worship.

Intercessions need to be prayed not read. This may be difficult for some members of the congregation to do, especially if it is the clergy who normally prepare the week's intercessions to tie in with the sermon. Lay people who have not composed the thanksgiving and petitionary prayers themselves may be tempted to read them as they would read a book or a memo from the vicar. If they are invited to intercede they could make sure that they get to church early, read the intercessions prayerfully to themselves, pray them, and then when the time comes to read them aloud try to make them a real but audible prayer. It is generally better, however, to invite those who are called to a public ministry of intercession to compose their own prayers for use at the Eucharist. Such prayers will need to be co-ordinated with the sermon and this is not always easy to achieve since priest and people are usually busy people. Lay people who regularly intercede at the Eucharist may need encouragement and training but the result will normally be that the prayers take on a new dimension of sincerity which will be noticeable. Sincere prayer is also infectious. Those who hear such prayers are moved to pray more deeply and sometimes more fervently themselves.

Throughout the Eucharist worshippers on earth are united with worshippers in heaven around the throne of God where Christ mediates for all. Intercession is not confined to a 'spot' in the service. It is an integral part of Christ's work throughout and it is by joining ourselves to him that we receive the fruits of his sacrifice on the cross in Holy Communion, either through receiving the bread and wine, the outward species of Christ's Body and Blood, or through spiritual communion with him.

Whether or nor Christians have a public ministry of petitionary prayer, all are called to pray. Those who plead with God on other people's behalf over a period of many years may develop such confidence in Christ's victory and saving power that they become united with Christ and full of joy. Such people look like everyone else, they cry like everyone else, they even look unhappy at times, but they carry in themselves a deep well of water, the water of eternal life. They

have drunk of that water themselves: 'Those who drink of the water
that I will give them will never be thirsty. The water that I will give
them will become in them a spring of water gushing up to eternal life'
(John 4.14). Such people cannot be found on every street corner, but
many of them can be discovered if one takes the trouble to look for
them. They are the holy ones of God, the ones in whom no boundaries
can be found because they have been consumed by Love. They have
become reservoirs of God's love. Being full of gratitude to God, full of
the fruit of the Spirit, full of overflowing love, their joy knows no
bounds. Love, peace and joy spill over into other people's lives.

People will gravitate to them without fully understanding why they
are attracted to them. They simply go away feeling more compassionate
and loving towards others, more at peace with themselves and their
circumstances, more joyful and thankful, more inspired to keep
searching for union with God themselves.

Among Christians it is easy to find examples of these kinds of people
throughout history. Perhaps one will suffice. When St Seraphim was a
very old man he stopped being a hermit. By this time Christ had
overcome all self-seeking and self-indulgence in him. He had become
full of the fruit of the Spirit. He was totally God-centred. He radiated
joy. Guided by the Holy Spirit and by the Virgin Mary, for whom he
had great love and devotion, he became a source of healing and peace to
those whom he now received freely at the doors of his monastery cell at
Sarov in Russia. His encounter with Nicholas Motilov, when Motilov
looks into Seraphim's eyes and encounters the loveliness, peace,
sweetness, warmth and heavenly scent of God's love, is very well
known. It is used in the liturgy of his feast day in at least one Anglican
community.[2] Less well known, but equally important, is a subsequent
story about him.

One of his biographers, Iulia de Beausobre, writing in novel form,
comments that when he was near to death

> Joy was in his nature, Now through incessant effort, its enriched stream
> overflowed to all, reviving them. A life giving stream, it washed away all
> despondency and sorrow.[3]

One day he met two dejected novices. Feeling utterly miserable they
had tried to avoid contact with him, but he reached them before they
could turn aside. He knew at once what was wrong:

> Taking hold of their hands he called out, 'Away with despondency.
> There is nothing Christ has not conquered. Nothing.'

At his approach, their mood had calmed, and mirrored his. Their anguish was gone, and they smiled. Singing, he continued on his way, his thin white hair blowing in the cold wind. Dry leaves, caught in the fringes of the long green shawl, scraped the sand path behind him. The young men sighed, comforted. Returning, each to his cell, they prepared for a long night of vigil and of prayer.[4]

Yes, it is like that. We all need the encouragement of others who are older and wiser than we are, who know God and radiate his joy and self-offering love which is found at its height in the Eucharist.

While people like St Seraphim, St Thérèse of Lisieux and Blessed Faustina do attract and inspire some of us, they also repel and evoke acts of hatred in others. These saints of God would not stop their work for God even if it were to cost them their lives. We should not stop either, even if we find ourselves criticized, reviled and hated. This does not mean that we can be certain that we are doing God's work if we are under attack. Some people do feel more confident that they are doing their work well if they are being attacked by evil people, or by demons. That is a false premise. We cannot judge by that criterion, only by the fruit of our prayer.

There can be little doubt, however, that attack during prayer at the Eucharist, whether it comes from the dark and sinful aspect of our own personalities or from outside agencies, be they other human beings, earth-bound souls or evil spirits, does occur. The source is immaterial in one way. The remedy, as already indicated (see p. 79), is always to keep one's eyes fixed on Jesus and to walk through the miasma of evil knowing that one's soul cannot be harmed. Such attack is not uncommon. When it happens it adds to the intercessor's suffering because no one likes to experience conflict during this most holy of all worship services. Again, common sense, patience and a good sense of proportion will usually be all that is required.

The Eucharist is sometimes celebrated in connection with the ministry of deliverance. This may be done when a place has been cleansed of demons as a way of celebrating its restoration to peace. It is more commonly offered for human beings. When a man or woman has been freed from oppression, or even possession, by evil — whatever its source — he or she may need to be sealed in the Holy Spirit. The Eucharist is celebrated; the freed person may be offered the ministry of the laying on of hands and anointing, given Holy Communion and blessed.

In this book the ministry of deliverance has not been discussed in any depth, nor will it be. There is no doubt that this specialized form of intercessory ministry, accompanied by authoritative commands to dead souls or demons to 'depart to the place God has prepared for them and never return', has a place in the life of the Church. It is, however, a ministry that is best undertaken by specialists who know what they are doing and are authorized by the Church to undertake this work. Books about the subject abound, but no book can teach as much as direct contact with Christ. Those who are called by God to the ministry of deliverance are greatly helped by other people who are more experienced and who have the gift of discernment between good spirits and evil ones. It is a dangerous ministry, not to be undertaken lightly or ill-advisedly.

By contrast the ministry of blessing should be used much more widely than it is. Such a ministry should not be confined to bishops and presbyters. They, it is true, have the authority to bless people, places and things in the name of Christ and his Church, but those of us who are not priests can bring blessing to people and places by our very presence, by our prayers, by our sincere desire for their well-being and contact with God. The prayer 'God bless you', or 'May God bless you', can be real, sincere and a claim upon Christ's victory. To bless people in that way is to encircle them in God's love, to wish them the joy of knowing that they are drawn into the perpetual dance of love that is taking place between Father, Son and Holy Spirit. It is petition, thanksgiving and protection rolled into one. Lay people are often reluctant to think of themselves as Christ's ambassadors, bringers of his blessing to others, but they are, or can be, and they should rejoice whenever they are welcome and inspired to pray 'May God bless you'.

The call to intercession as a lifetime work is a call that comes to all Christians who share in Christ's ministry, that is, to all of us. Within that task there are some who will be called to focused prayer for healing, for reconciliation, for peace with justice, for unity. Christ's victory over sin, evil and death is assured. As we look forward to his second coming and say *Maranatha*, 'Amen. Come, Lord Jesus!' (Revelation 22.20), so we can also give thanks 'at all times and for everything in the name of our Lord Jesus Christ' (Ephesians 5.20), knowing in the depths of our heart that we can give thanks even before we ask.

Omega

Born in a
rain forest
I grew tall,
rich in sap
full in leaf;
shelter and home
to God's creatures,

until I was
wrenched
from the earth;
untimely
seized by
someone's need.
Greed, ignorance?
Who knows.

Hewn asunder,
fragmented,
manufactured
into goods
to be sold
to the rich,
I despaired.

Yet by chance
or by design?
God knows,
one fragment
of my torn body
fell into
loving hands,

There
to be shaped
hollowed out,
pierced,
ground smooth
and given
to be held
with love,

to remember
a life
emptied of self
hollowed out
in service;
sacrificed,
raised.

For this I
was born
to die.
By His life
and death
all creation
is made new.

Notes

Chapter 1

1 *Ginkgo biloba*, or the maidenhair tree, is the only surviving species of a group of coniferous trees that flourished in the Mesozoic era. It is thought to have been the first gymnospore to grow on earth. It was found growing in China; a specimen planted in 1762 can still be seen at the Royal Botanic Gardens, Kew, England.

2 Twenty-two species of trees, their characteristics and uses, are noted in the *New Bible Dictionary* (2nd edn; London and Downers Grove, IL: Inter-Varsity Press, 1982), pp. 1215–17.

3 Cf. Isaiah 18.5; Ezekiel 15.1–8.

4 Candles are increasingly used in prayer by members of all Christian denominations. They are symbols of Christ, the light of the world, Christ who is ever present.

5 For Orthodox Christians and for many others, holy icons that are painted in prayer and blessed by a bishop are more than holy pictures; they contain the real presence of Christ.

6 Prayers are offered at the shrine of St Melangell in Pennant Melangell, Powys, each day at 9.00 am and many people unite themselves with the guardian of the shrine in this way.

7 Millions of people of all faiths join in this prayer by Satish Kumar for world peace:

Lead me from darkness to light,
   from fear to trust,
   from war to peace.
Let peace fill our hearts, our world, our universe.

8 Julian of Norwich, *Enfolded in Love,* tr. members of the Julian Shrine in Norwich (London: Darton, Longman and Todd, 1980), p. 3.

9 William Shakespeare, *As You Like It*, II.i.12.

10 William Blake, 'Auguries of Innocence'; quoted from *Oxford Book of Mystical Verse*, ed. D. H. S. Nicholson and A. H. E. Lee (Oxford: Oxford University Press, 1927), p. 105.

11 David Jones, *Vexilla Regis*, drawn in October 1947; exhibited in Kettle's Yard, Cambridge. This passage is taken from his commentary in a letter to Mrs Ede: Catalogue, *David Jones, Drawings and Paintings*, p. 114. See also Merlin James, *David Jones 1895–1974: A Map of the Artist's Mind* (London: Lund Humphries, 1995), p. 44.

12 Joshua Smith, *Divine Hymns or Spiritual Songs* (New Hampshire, 1784), verses 1–2.

Chapter 2

1   Tertullian, *De cultu feminarum*; in J. P. Migne (ed.), *Patrologia Latina* (Paris, 1844), vol. 1, cols 304–305.
2   Augustine, *On the Holy Trinity,* tr. A. W. Hadden and W. G. T. Shedd in *Select Library of Nicene Fathers* (Buffalo, 1887), vol. III, p. 159.
3   R.P. Henri Petitot OP, *Ste Thérèse de Lisieux. Une renaissance spirituelle* (Paris, 1925), p. 266; cited in Ida Friederike Görres, *The Hidden Face* (London: Burns & Oates, 1959), p. 357.
4   Ibid., p. 359.
5   Julian of Norwich, *Enfolded in Love*, p. 39.
6   Walter Wink, *The Powers and the Life of the Spirit* (Minneapolis: Augsburg Fortress, 1992), p. 298.
7   Ibid., pp. 307–8.
8   Julian of Norwich, *Enfolded in Love*, p. 64.

Chapter 3

1   See *New Bible Dictionary*, p. 1216.
2   John Robinson, *Honest to God* (London: SCM Press, 1963).
3   *The Life of St Teresa*, tr. J. M. Cohen (Harmondsworth: Penguin Books, 1957).
4   Baron von Hügel, *Essays and Addresses* (2nd series; London, 1930), VIII, p. 240.
5   Iulia de Beausobre, *Creative Suffering* (London: A. & C. Black/Westminster: Dacre Press, 1940), pp. 28–9.
6   Ibid., p. 29.
7   St Thérèse of Lisieux, *The Story of a Soul*; tr. Ronald Knox, *The Autobiography of a Saint* (London: Harvill Press, 1958).
8   Prayer in *Oxford Book of Prayer*, ed. George Appleton (Oxford: Oxford University Press, 1985), p. 107; originally published in *Morning Noon and Night*, ed. John Carden (1976).

Chapter 4

1   Anon., *Dream of the Rood*; in *Earliest English Poems*, tr. and ed. Michael Alexander (Harmondsworth: Penguin, 1966), p. 107.
2   Ibid.
3   The Ruthwell Cross stands in the parish church, a few miles from the Solway Firth. It is a stone cross, more than five metres high, and was erected during the lifetime of the Venerable Bede. On its sides is carved part of the *Dream of the Rood*.
4   Michael Alexander, 'Ancient witness to the Crucifixion', *The Tablet* (6/13 April 1996), p. 460.
5   *New Bible Dictionary*, pp. 253–4.

6   See Mary Craig, *Candles in the Dark* (London: Spire/Hodder & Stoughton, 1984), pp. 104–38, 226–61.

7   Maria Tarnawska, *Blessed Sister Faustina* (London: Veritas Publication Centre, 1993), p. 190.

8   Ibid., p. 191.

9   Ibid., p. 301.

10 *Dream of the Rood*, p. 108.

11 See Olivier Clément, *Sources* (Paris: Editions Stock, 1982); English edn, *The Roots of Christian Mysticism* (2nd edn: London: New City, 1993), pp. 76–91 for a full exposition of the human vocation.

12 Hesychasm is the system of mysticism propounded by the monks of Mount Athos in the fourteenth century. Hesychast theology distinguishes between God's essence and his 'energy'. It teaches that human beings can attain to a mystical vision of God's energy but not to his essence. Some Western theologians would oppose this distinction and say that God's essence is the object of the Beatific vision. Symeon of Studion, the 'New Theologian', is the father of the movement; Gregory Palamas is its most outstanding defender. It is now associated with Orthodoxy, though in the sixteenth and seventeenth centuries the influence of Western theologians caused the doctrine to be dropped from the Russian Orthodox Church of that time.

13 Basil of Caesarea, quoted by Gregory Nazianzen, *Eulogy of St Basil the Great (Oration* 43), 48.

14 Irenaeus of Lyons, *Against Heresies*, III, 10, 2.

15 Gregory of Nyssa, *Against Apollinarius*, 2.

16 Olivier Clément, *Roots of Christian Mysticism,* p. 265.

17 Ibid., p. 267.

18 See note 12 above.

19 This phrase is meant to refer to panentheism, not to pantheism. 'The Being of God includes and penetrates the whole universe so that every part of it exists in Him, but His Being is more than, and is not exhausted by, the universe': *The Oxford Dictionary of the Christian Church*, ed. F. L. Cross (London, New York and Toronto: Oxford University Press, 1957), p. 1010.

20 *Dream of the Rood,* p. 107.

21 Iulia de Beausobre, *Flame in the Snow* (Constable, 1945), p. 140.

22 Ibid.

23 Ibid., p. 157.

Chapter 5

1   See 'Dead Sea Scrolls' in *New Bible Dictionary*, p. 272.

2   Iulia de Beausobre, *Flame in the Snow*, pp. 153–4.

3   Isaac of Nineveh, *Ascetic Treatises*; quoted in Olivier Clément, *Roots of Christian Mysticism*, p. 253.

4   Maximus the Confessor, *Ambigua*, 7; *Roots of Christian Mysticism*, p. 267.

5   Maximus the Confessor, *Gnostic Centuries*, II, 28; *Roots of Christian Mysticism*, p. 267.

6   Ibid., p. 269.
7   A fuller exposition of this theme can be found in Una Kroll, *Vocation to Resistance* (London: Darton, Longman and Todd, 1995), pp. 137–53.
8   Adrienne von Speyr, *Confession*, tr. Douglas W. Stott (San Francisco: Ignatius Press, 1960), p. 140.
9   See *Brewer's Dictionary of Phrase and Fable*, ed. Ivor H. Evans (14th edn; London: Cassell, 1989), p. 1022.
10 I heard Gonville Ffrench-Beytagh speak about this at a private meeting about apartheid in London in 1974.
11 Terry Waite, speaking on his release.
12 Elizabeth Jennings, *Times and Seasons* (Manchester: Carcanet, 1992), p. 45.
13 Little Sister Magdeleine of Jesus, *Jesus Is the Master of the Impossible* (Edition Le Livre Ouvert, 1991), p. 33.
14 Ibid., p. 35.
15 See above, Chapter 1, note 11, p. 123.
16 Gerald Hudson, 'Gethsemane' (unpublished).

Chapter 6

1   Information about the pomegranate tree has been gathered from two main sources: *New Bible Dictionary*, p. 1216; and Meinrad Craighead, *The Sign of the Tree* (London: Mitchell Beazley, 1979), p. 86.
2   Revelation 22.2 KJV and RSV; in some versions, notably the New Jerusalem Bible, the trees line the banks of the river, just as they appear in Ezekiel.
3   2 Esdras 8.52–56.
4   I met Sadie Patterson at a Youth Rally in the Albert Hall in 1974 and learnt about her work.
5   After the McGuire children were killed on 10 August 1976, their aunt Mairead Corrigan, Betty Williams and Ciaran McKeown founded the Peace People; thousands joined their marches for peace in 1976. See Ray Davey, *A Channel of Peace* (Northampton: Marshall Pickering, 1993), pp. 126–7.
6   Quoted in Alf McCreary, *Corrymeela: Hill of Harmony* (New York: Hawthorne Books, 1976), p. 24.
7   Ibid., p. 40.
8   During the internment crisis in 1971 large numbers of children were evacuated from Belfast by Corrymeela workers. Local groups were formed to foster the Corrymeela spirit in areas where sectarian hatred was the norm.
9   Alf McCreary, *Corrymeela*, caption to photograph between pp. 40 and 41.
10 For a full description of Glencree see Brian Frost, *Women and Forgiveness* (London: Collins Fount, 1990), pp. 13–56.
11 Tr. the monks of St Bernard's Abbey, Coalville, Leicester; published in *The Tablet* (8 June 1996), p. 749.
12 Ibid.
13 For the cost of such work to one individual who lived and died for Christian Unity see Brian Frost, *Glastonbury Journey: Marjorie Milne's Search for Reconciliation* (London: Becket/Mowbray, 1986).

14 Foreword by Jean Vanier to Kathryn Spink, *The Call of the Desert* (London: Darton, Longman and Todd, 1993), p. ix.

15 See Père René Voillaume, *Brothers of Men* (London: Darton, Longman and Todd, 1966).

16 See René Bazin, *Charles de Foucauld: Hermit and Explorer*, tr. Peter Keelan (London: Burns, Oates and Washbourne, 1923); and Elizabeth Hamilton, *The Desert My Dwelling Place* (London: Hodder and Stoughton, 1968).

17 Kathryn Spink, *The Call of the Desert*, p. 230.

18 Ibid., pp. 114–15; see also pp. 230–1.

19 Ibid., p. 114.

20 In July 1972.

21 Personal experience at Cambridge University, 1944.

22 See Pope John Paul II, Apostolic Letter *Tertio Millennio Adveniente* (24 November 1994) and Encyclical Letter *Ut Unum Sint*; and Br Eoin de Bhaldraithe, letter, *The Tablet* (29 June 1996), p. 856.

23 Isaac of Nineveh, *Ascetic Treatises*; quoted in Olivier Clément, *The Roots of Christian Mysticism*, p. 278.

24 Ibid., p. 283.

25 Irenaeus of Lyons, *Against Heresies*, V, 7, 1; *Roots of Christian Mysticism*, p. 265.

26 Cyril of Alexandria, *Treasures*, 33; *Roots of Christian Mysticism*, p. 264.

27 Maximus the Confessor, *Centuries on Charity*, III, 52; *Roots of Christian Mysticism*, p. 265.

Chapter 7

1 Joni Eareckson Tada, *Start of a Journey* (London: Marshall Pickering, 1980; reissued 1991), p. 98.

2 Ibid., p. 112.

3 Ibid., p. 118.

4 See Coretta King, *My Life with Martin Luther King* (London: Hodder and Stoughton, 1970); Trevor Huddleston, *Naught for Your Comfort* (London and Glasgow: Collins, 1956); etc.

5 See *Long Walk to Freedom: The Autobiography of Nelson Mandela* (London: Little, Brown, 1994).

6 Valentin Zander, *St Seraphim of Sarov*, tr. Sr Gabriel Anne SSC (London: SPCK, 1975), p. x.

7 Mary Craig, *Candles in the Dark* (London: Hodder and Stoughton/Spire, 1984), p. 195.

8 Ibid., p. 196.

9 Ibid.

10 Ibid., p. 201.

11 Ibid., p. 212.

Chapter 8

1   Book of Common Prayer, Preface to the Eucharistic prayer.
2   Iulia de Beausobre, *Flame in the Snow*, p. 148; Valentin Zander, *St Seraphim*. Also quoted in Una Kroll, *Vocation to Resistance*, p. 147. This passage is in use at Tymawr Convent, Lydart, Gwent.
3   Iulia de Beausobre, *Flame in the Snow*, p. 155.
4   Ibid., pp. 155–6.